THE
KOREAN
WAR

KOREAN WAR

INTERPRETING PRIMARY DOCUMENTS

Dennis Nishi, Book Editor

Daniel Leone, President
Bonnie Szumski, Publisher
Scott Barbour, Managing Editor

**GREENHAVEN
PRESS®**

THOMSON

San Diego • Detroit • New York • San Francisco • Cleveland
New Haven, Conn. • Waterville, Maine • London • Munich

LIBRARY OF CONGRESS CATALOGING-IN-PUBLICATION DATA
The Korean War : interpreting primary documents / Dennis Nishi, book editor.
p. cm.
Includes bibliographical references and index.
ISBN 0-7377-1201-5 (pbk. : alk. paper) — ISBN 0-7377-1202-3 (lib. : alk. paper)
1. Korean War, 1950–1953. 2. World politics—1945–1955. I. Nishi, Dennis, 1967–
DS918 .K5648 2003
951.904'2—dc21   2002040890

CONTENTS

Chapter 2: The Korean War and the World

Chapter 3: We Were There: A Personal Perspective of Korea

FOREWORD

In a debate on the nature of the historian's task, the Canadian intellectual Michael Ignatieff wrote, "I don't think history is a lesson in patriotism. It should be a lesson in truth. And the truth is both painful and many-sided." Part of Ignatieff's point was that those who seek to understand the past should guard against letting prejudice or patriotism interfere with the truth. This point, although simple, is subtle. Everyone would agree that patriotism is no excuse for outright fabrication, and that prejudice should never induce a historian to deliberately lie or deceive. Ignatieff's concern, however, was not so much with deliberate falsification as it was with the way prejudice and patriotism can lead to selective perception, which can skew the judgment of even those who are sincere in their efforts to understand the past. The truth, especially about the how and why of historical events, is seldom simple, and those who wish to genuinely understand the past must be sensitive to its complexities.

Each of the anthologies in the Greenhaven Press Interpreting Primary Documents series strives to portray the events and attitudes of the past in all their complexity. Rather than providing a simple narrative of the events, each volume presents a variety of views on the issues and events under discussion and encourages the student to confront and examine the complexity that attends the genuine study of history.

Furthermore, instead of aiming simply to transmit information from historian to student, the series is designed to develop and train students to become historians themselves, by focusing on the interpretation of primary documents. Such documents, including newspaper articles, speeches, personal reflections, letters, diaries, memoranda, and official reports, are the raw material from which the historian refines an authentic understanding of the past. The anthology examining desegregation, for instance, includes the voices of presidents, state governors, and ordinary citizens, and draws from the *Congressional Record,* newspapers and magazines, letters, and books published at the time. The selections differ in scope and opinion as well, allowing the student to examine the issue of desegregation from a variety of perspectives. By looking frankly at the arguments offered by those in favor of racial segregation and by those opposed, for example, students can better understand those arguments, the people who advanced them, and the time in which they lived.

The structure of each book in the Interpreting Primary Documents series helps readers sharpen the critical faculties the serious study of history requires. A concise introduction outlines the era or event at hand and provides the necessary historical background. The chapters themselves begin with a preface containing a straightforward account of the events discussed and an overview of how these events can be interpreted in different ways by examining the different documents in the chapter. The selections, in turn, are chosen for their accessibility and relevance, and each is preceded by a short introduction offering historical context and a summary of the author's point of view. A set of questions to guide interpretation accompanies each article and encourages readers to examine the authors' prejudices, probe their assumptions, and compare and contrast the various perspectives offered in the chapter. Finally, a detailed timeline traces the development of key events, a comprehensive bibliography of selected secondary material guides further research, and a thorough index lets the reader quickly access relevant information.

As Ignatieff remarked, in the same debate in which he urged the historian to favor truth over blind patriotism, "History for me is the study of arguments." The Interpreting Primary Documents series is for readers eager to understand the arguments, and attitudes, that animated historical change.

INTRODUCTION

The Korean War began on June 25, 1950, when soldiers from Communist-ruled North Korea invaded the Republic of South Korea. The conflict was primarily a civil war, but it also involved twenty-three different nations as well as the United States and China. It was considered one of the bloodiest conflicts in history and resulted in 4 million military and civilian casualties. But despite the scope of the conflict, Korea has often been called America's forgotten war. It earned this distinction because it was fought between two wars that historically overshadowed it, World War II and Vietnam. It was also the first war the United States ever failed to conclusively win, which gave many Americans a reason to want to forget it. Regardless of its unpopularity, the Korean War was a pivotal event in world history. It was the first actual violent struggle in the Cold War between communism and democracy. It also signaled a change in roles for the United States, which would abandon its isolationist traditions and attempt to succeed wartorn Britain as the global peacekeeper. The new role would not only change the way the United States fought wars, but it also changed the way future wars would be defined. The Korean War, for example, was not officially acknowledged as a war at all. President Harry Truman knew he needed to act quickly and called it a police action so he could get around the need for congressional consent. He used this distinction and the authority of a UN Security Council resolution to send U.S. troops to help the South Koreans. Author Bevin Alexander writes, "Thus was born an unfortunate presidential precedent to try to sanitize and minimize American military actions by avoiding formal congressional declarations of war. This course had been followed by every American president since Truman."[1]

There was no doubt among those who fought and died

in Korea that it was a full-scale war. The fighting was just as involved and bitter as any past conflict. What made Korea different was its limited objectives. The United States had historically regarded war as a crusade between good and evil. The goal in fighting had always been to achieve a total victory over the enemy. But total victory in Korea risked drawing the Soviet Union (which was already indirectly involved) into the conflict. And once the Soviet Union had developed its own atomic weapons, every foreign policy decision now had to take that into account. Korea was not deemed worth the risk of another world war, especially if it became a nuclear one. Omar Bradley, chairman of the Joint Chiefs of Staff, called Korea "the wrong war, at the wrong place, at the wrong time, and with the wrong enemy."[2] Unfortunately for Korea, it became a pawn in a bigger cold war between two superpowers.

The Beginning of the Cold War
At the end of World War II, much of Europe had been devastated by the fighting. The cost in human life and property was incalculable and would take years to rebuild. The United States, which safely sat an ocean away, emerged from the war nearly unscathed. Its economy and industry, though drained, was quickly able to transition to peacetime production. Mass unemployment, which was predicted to occur after the demobilization of the military, never happened. In fact, the U.S. economy grew. The American people spent money with newfound confidence on products like radios, televisions, and cars. There was even a housing boom, which was fueled by the availability of affordable mortgages for returning servicemen. But it was far from a perfect world. A new threat to this prosperous way of life emerged that no other nation except the United States had the resources to counter.

The Soviet Union, a former ally, had become an enemy of Western democracy. One of the reasons for this hostility was the difference in the way both nations believed people should be governed. The Soviet Communist Party, led by

Joseph Stalin, ruled a totalitarian government that centrally controlled all aspects of the economy as well as its citizens' lives. Property and land was owned by the state, and resources were distributed to the people by the government. The American system of capitalist democracy functioned in the opposite way, emphasizing individual freedom, private ownership, and a free-market economy. Both sides believed their way of life was superior, and both sides believed the other was trying to dominate the world.

Containment Policy

One of the first gestures that put the Western allies on the defensive was the Soviet Union's formation of the Eastern Bloc. After World War II, the Soviet Union tightened its grip on a weakened Eastern Europe. Its army, which still occupied the nations it had liberated, helped Communist factions within these governments rise to power. Although the new republics were technically still independent nations, they answered directly to Moscow. This ring of protective satellite nations provided collective security and prevented any country adjoining Russia from being used as a staging area for an invasion. Former British prime minister Winston Churchill called this shield an iron curtain and warned that the West needed to remain vigilant. Author Robert Kelley writes that it was an understandably defensive move prompted by Russia's turbulent history:

> Russia is an ancient country that has been invaded again and again in its long history. . . . Consequently, the Russians were not in 1945 a trusting people. . . . The Russians have felt surrounded by enemies since long before the Communist revolution took place under V.I. Lenin in 1917. In 1945, much of the USSR lay in shattered, smoking ruins, and the Soviets were determined to guarantee their future military security by their own efforts, not by trusting others.[3]

The Western allies shared Churchill's views and saw it as

the beginning of the Soviet Union's push to expand communism globally. This perception was reinforced by Stalin's broken promise to help postwar Eastern Europe develop free nations. President Truman, who saw communism to be as much of a threat to the world as Nazi Germany, adopted the hard-line stance of advisers such as George Kennan, a State Department expert on Soviet affairs. Kennan believed the Soviet Union was an implacable foe whose expansionist tendencies needed to be contained. He advocated a patient but firm hand as opposed to a direct confrontation.

This new foreign policy was first put to the test in 1947. Great Britain, which formerly controlled a colonial empire that helped maintain order worldwide, announced that it could no longer provide assistance to Greece and Turkey. The governments of both nations had been weakened by the war and were being threatened by a Communist takeover. Truman appeared before Congress to request $400 million in aid to help these two threatened democracies. He was able to successfully convey the peril communism posed worldwide in the following speech:

> The seeds of totalitarian regimes are nurtured by misery and want. They spread and grow in the evil soil of poverty and strife. They reach their full growth when the hope of a people for a better life has died. We must keep that policy of the United States to support free peoples who are resisting attempted subjugation by armed minorities or by outside pressures.[4]

The Truman Doctrine was created to assist the rest of Western Europe, which faced the same threat as Turkey and Greece. It offered military and economic assistance to help stabilize fragile economies. The Marshall Plan went a step further by encouraging nations to work together to decide how to administer the aid. Secretary of State George Marshall, who authored the plan, even offered to help the Soviet Union and its allies. But Stalin refused, believing it was a thinly disguised plot to control Europe.

The Cold War Heats Up

The Cold War continued for years, but the first major confrontation took place in 1948. After Germany was defeated, the country was divided into occupation zones. The United States, Russia, France, and Britain each held a separate zone as well as a part of the German capital, Berlin—however, Berlin resided deep within the Soviet zone. The three Western powers consolidated their separate zones and established a democratic government. This angered Soviet premier Joseph Stalin, who did not want a bastion of democracy inside a Communist state. Stalin blocked all supply routes into Berlin in hopes the Western allies would leave rather than risk an armed confrontation. The United States, Britain, and France refused to back down or allow the people of the city to starve. They instead devised an elaborate plan to go over the heads of Soviet troops. Food, fuel, medicines, and other vital supplies were brought into the city by airplanes. The massive airlift continued for eleven months before Stalin withdrew his troops.

The success was a black eye for the Soviet Union and a victory for the West. It allowed the Western allies to take a firm stand against the Soviets without having to fight or appease them. Truman later assured the security of Western Europe by creating a mutual defense pact that could counter the Soviet Union and its satellite nations. It was called the North Atlantic Treaty Organization (NATO). Twelve nations joined under the agreement that an attack on one was an attack on all members. Soviet premier Stalin accused the Western allies of aggressive intent and objected to the alliance. But two Communist victories later that year would shift the balance of power again.

On August 29, 1949, the Soviet Union detonated its first atomic bomb, which meant the United States no longer held a monopoly on atomic weapons. The second victory was the overthrow of U.S.-sponsored Chiang Kai-shek and the Nationalist government in China. After years of civil war, militant Communists succeeded in establishing the new People's Republic of China. Chiang Kai-shek fled to

Formosa (now known as Taiwan), an island one hundred miles off the southeastern coast of mainland China. Party chairman Mao Zedong (also spelled Tse-tung) was appointed premier of the new Communist state. The Soviet Union immediately recognized the new government and established a mutual defense pact. This was a major blow to the United States because it placed a powerful new enemy in the middle of Asia and on the border of Korea.

A History of Occupation

Korea lies on a peninsula that extends south from China. It has one of the oldest civilizations in history, which is rich in tradition and culture. But Korea also has a history of invasion by its neighbors. After 1876, Korea became the object of rivalry among competing colonial powers as well. Japan and Russia eventually went to war over control of Korea and Manchuria. Japan was able to defeat Russia's army in the Far East and was given control of Korea in the peace settlement. Japan ruled the colony harshly and exploited its resources and labor until the Japanese were defeated in 1945. But even after being liberated, Korea would still not gain independence. During the Cairo Conference two years before, the Allies had determined that Korea would be free and independent only after a thirty- or forty-year period of trusteeship. It was thought that Korea would have to learn to govern itself again after being occupied by Japan for so long. Unfortunately, these plans were upset by the conflicting agendas of the two occupying nations and the division of the country.

Korea Is Divided

The decision to divide Korea was the result of an agreement made between the United States and the Soviet Union during the final stages of World War II. U.S. president Franklin Roosevelt, British prime minister Winston Churchill, and Soviet premier Joseph Stalin had met at the Yalta Conference to finalize war plans and determine the fate of postwar Europe. Roosevelt's main intention also included bringing the Soviet Union into the war against Japan. U.S. military planners believed the final defeat of Japan would be a long and difficult campaign. Stalin agreed to help, but historians believe it was not out of any sense of solidarity between the two nations. They believe Stalin was anxious to get a share of the Japanese empire.

It was finally agreed that the Soviet Union would receive control of the Kuril Islands and Sakhalin Island (both of which reside between Russia and Japan) and part of Manchuria. Bringing the Soviet Union into the Pacific turned out to be a mistake since Japan was closer to defeat than anybody realized. When the Soviet Union declared war on Japan, the first atomic bomb had already been dropped on Hiroshima. The Japanese surrendered a few days after the second bomb was dropped on Nagasaki. The Red Army followed through with its agreement and invaded Manchuria. It gave all the heavy equipment it captured from the Japanese to the Communists who were fighting the Nationalist government in China. Soviet troops also entered the northern tip of Korea, which prompted the United States to take action. With the sudden collapse of the Japanese empire, the United States realized there was nothing to stop the Soviet Union from taking over the entire country and creating another Soviet satellite. U.S. troops were sent into the south of Korea, and a plan was presented to create two separate occupational zones. Korea was then unceremoniously divided at the thirty-eighth parallel. The dividing line was an arbitrary decision, chosen because it conveniently divided the nation in half on a map. It was meant to be temporary, but neither side could come up with a mutually acceptable plan to unify the country.

The UN declared that national elections should be held to allow the people of Korea to choose what form of government they wanted. But the Soviet Union sealed the borders and refused to allow elections in the North. They were afraid the Communists would be driven out. On May 10, 1948, the South Koreans established the Republic of Korea

(ROK) and elected Syngman Rhee as president three months later. In response to the elections in the South, the Communists established the Democratic People's Republic on September 9 and appointed Kim Il Sung the premier of North Korea. Both governments claimed control over the entire peninsula, but the UN only recognized South Korea as the legitimate national government.

By 1948 the United States and the Soviet Union had pulled most of their troops out of Korea. The Soviets left behind advisers and a well-trained and well-equipped North Korean army. The United States left a small team of advisers but no heavy equipment since it did not trust Syngman Rhee. Rhee had become very vocal in his condemnation of the North's Communist government, and the United States ironically believed Rhee might try to reunify North Korea by force if he had the means. The first priority of the United States was to withdraw despite the warnings of top military advisers about the growing threat North Korea posed. Europe was a bigger priority, writes Secretary of State Omar Bradley, and Korea had been excluded from the U.S. defense perimeter in Asia: "We had occupied Korea but we did not want to stay any longer than we had to. As a military operations zone, Korea—mountainous and bitterly cold in the winter—had no appeal. In the very remote event we would be compelled to launch military operations on the Asiatic mainland, Korea would certainly be bypassed."[5]

The Invasion of South Korea

The North Korean People's Army (NKPA) invaded South Korea on June 25, 1950. The NKPA attacked with ninety thousand men, a number of whom were seasoned troops with combat experience in the Chinese and Soviet armies during World War II. The NKPA also had 126 Soviet-built T34 tanks, against which the ROK had no defense. ROK forces guarding the border, a third of which were on leave, were taken by surprise and quickly overrun. The South Korean capital of Seoul was captured within three days.

Truman believed all Communist moves worldwide were dictated directly by the Soviet Union. But Nikita Khrushchev, secretary of the Central Committee, contended that Kim Il Sung devised the invasion plan on his own and then traveled to Moscow to get approval. Stalin and Mao Zedong were lukewarm about the plan and worried that an assault might elicit an American response. Mao Zedong was especially concerned that the United States would extend its crusade to engage a war with China. The two leaders reluctantly agreed after Kim assured them that the battle could be won in three days. U.S. diplomat Charles E. Bohlen, an expert on Soviet affairs, refutes the possibility that the Soviet Union did not play a key role in the invasion:

There are those who now say that the war was not started by the Soviet Union but by an independent act of the North Koreans. This is childish nonsense. How could an army, trained in every respect by the Soviet Union, with Soviet advisors at every level, and utterly dependent on Moscow for supplies, move without Soviet authorization? Stalin would not have been so careless as to permit the North Koreans to kick off a war that conceivably might involve the Soviet Union in a confrontation with the United States. The Soviet Union has never joked about war.[6]

Although the United States had officially written off Korea, the invasion prompted Washington to quickly change its policy toward Asia. Truman believed a show of strength was the only way to respond to the Communists. Anything less than a firm response would be regarded as appeasement. Truman authorized a naval blockade and air strikes south of the thirty-eighth parallel in support of ROK forces. He also redirected the Seventh Fleet into the Formosa Strait to discourage a widening of the hostilities by the Communist Chinese. The conflict in Korea could provide a good opportunity for Mao Zedong to sneak across the strait and crush the Nationalists once and for all.

Truman's War

Up to this point, Truman had made the decision to send military aid to Korea without the approval of Congress or the American people. MacArthur, who had always believed the Cold War would be won or lost in Asia, brazenly flew to South Korea and made his assessment of the situation from the front lines. He reported that the South Koreans would be defeated in weeks without U.S. help. Truman approved the request for ground troops the following day.

Task Force Smith was sent in to stop the NPKA advance until the rest of the Eighth Army could be sent. The unit of 406 men was scrounged from the occupation force in Japan. Like their South Korean counterparts, most of these soldiers had no combat experience, very little training, and were ill equipped to handle tanks. When Task Force Smith arrived, it was only able to delay the North Korean advance for seven hours before being completely routed. U.S. and South Korean forces were eventually driven all the way back to the southeastern city of Pusan, the port city where they had originally landed.

Operation Chromite

UN troops regrouped at the Naktong River and established a defensive line called the Pusan Perimeter around the cities of Taegu and Pusan. With the ocean at their backs and retreat impossible, the standing order given was to defend their positions at all costs. Fortunately, troops and supplies had been steadily arriving in Pusan and increased the combined strength of allied forces to ninety-two thousand men. With the help of airpower, which disrupted the long supply lines of the North Korean army, UN forces were able to hold the line.

Once MacArthur was assured the Pusan Perimeter was stable, he proposed a daring amphibious landing at the western port city of Inchon. It was far behind enemy lines and, if successful, would cut the North Korean army in half. But the landing was risky because it required precise timing. The channel access to the port was narrow and in-

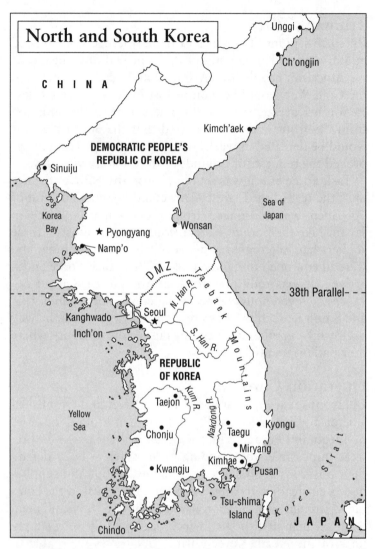

North and South Korea

CHINA

DEMOCRATIC PEOPLE'S
REPUBLIC OF KOREA

Unggi

Ch'ongjin

Kimch'aek

Sinuiju

Korea
Bay

★ Pyongyang

Namp'o

Wonsan

Sea of
Japan

D M Z

N. Han R.

Taebaek

38th Parallel

Kanghwado

Inch'on

Seoul

S. Han R.

Mountains

REPUBLIC
OF KOREA

Taejon

Kum R.

Nakdong R.

Yellow
Sea

Chonju

Taegu

Kyongu

Miryang

Kwangju

Kimhae

Pusan

Korea Strait

Tsu-shima
Island

Chindo

JAPAN

accessible at low tide. The mouth of the port was guarded
by Wolmindo (Moon Tip) Island, and the city itself was
protected by a high sea wall. MacArthur assured the Joint
Chiefs of Staff (the senior leaders for all branches of the
armed services) that these were the reasons the enemy
would never anticipate a landing at Inchon. It was a strategy MacArthur had successfully employed during World

War II, "being where the enemy ain't."[7] The landing was named Operation Chromite, and it worked exactly as MacArthur had hoped. UN forces met very little resistance from the surprised North Koreans. With the help of a heavy screen of artillery and airpower, there were only 174 allied casualties. MacArthur's success in capturing Inchon signaled the Eighth Army to break out of the Pusan Perimeter. The two forces advanced toward each other in a pincer movement. After a week of intense fighting, the battered North Korea army fled north in retreat.

A New Phase of the War

By September, UN forces had recaptured Seoul and NKPA troops had been driven back over the thirty-eighth parallel. The UN had achieved its original goal of repelling the invaders. But MacArthur wanted to cross the border and finish the job. The United States had actually considered reunifying the country since the beginning of the war. The major concern it faced was how the Soviet Union and China would react to the invasion of North Korea. Author David Rees writes that it was an unprecedented opportunity:

> The fear of Chinese or Soviet intervention was outweighed by the desire to exploit the victory politically, to realize the hopes expressed during the Naktong fighting for the unification of Korea. . . . Even more pressing was the need to exploit the situation militarily, and to destroy completely the People's Army, even if it did mean moving across the parallel.[8]

MacArthur was granted permission to cross the thirty-eighth parallel but was limited from entering the northeast region of the country. Truman did not want to risk border clashes that could provoke China or the Soviet Union. Emboldened by his recent victories, MacArthur accepted his orders and defiantly added that he regarded all of Korea to be open for military operations. Truman and the Joint Chiefs did not respond to this statement, which may have been acknowledged by MacArthur as consent. This turned out to be a mistake and would result in changing the course of the war.

UN forces crossed the thirty-eighth parallel on October 1. They quickly captured three coastal cities and the North Korean capital of Pyongyong by October 19. China, which had been nervously watching the war close on its border, warned the United States against advancing any farther. Mao Zedong had made it clear that he would not tolerate an enemy state (a unified democratic Korea) so close to his border. Mao was one of a long line of Chinese rulers who had used Korea as a buffer against invaders. This official statement by the Communist Party summarized the danger UN forces presented to national security:

> The situation today is very clear. The U.S. imperialists are copying the old trick of the Japanese bandits— first invading Korea and then invading China. Everyone knows that Korea is a small country, but that its strategic position is very important. Just as with the Japanese imperialists in the past, the main objective of the U.S. aggression on Korea is not Korea itself, but China. History shows us that the existence of the Korean People's Republic and its fall and the security or danger of China are closely intertwined. The one cannot be safeguarded without the other. . . . To save our neighbor is to save ourselves.[9]

The United States dismissed the threat as a bluff. It mistakenly assumed that China was just another satellite nation under the thumb of the Soviet Union and would not act independently. And military planners believed the Soviet Union would not intervene at this point of the war, especially since it had already passed up more opportune times such as at Pusan. Unfortunately, MacArthur and the United States had seriously misjudged the situation. China intended to do more than saber rattle. A large number of troops from Manchuria were sent across the Yalu River in mid-October.

Since they had no vehicles, rarely used roads, and mostly traveled at night, they were able to enter Korea undetected.

The first clashes between Chinese and UN troops occurred on October 25, fifty miles south of the border. The Chinese attacked the UN forces across a wide front before suddenly withdrawing back into the mountains. It is not known why the Chinese withdrew, though some historians theorize the attack was a warning to the UN. Others believe the Chinese were trying to lure MacArthur into an ambush. MacArthur himself surmised that the Chinese had fought themselves out and were in retreat. He was so confident victory could be achieved in one final thrust that he told his troops they would be home before Christmas if the operation was successful. The statement was leaked to the press, and it became known as the "Home by Christmas Offensive."

On November 26 the Chinese attacked in force with over three hundred thousand men. They completely surprised the overextended and outnumbered UN forces, which had been divided into two flanking columns. The Chinese infiltrated the gap between the two groups and attacked their flanks. UN forces were driven back in an unprecedented three-hundred-mile retreat, the longest in U.S. military history. Over fifteen hundred UN troops had to be evacuated out of the eastern ports of Hungnam and Wonsan.

The Limited War

After the UN's disastrous rout, a flustered MacArthur informed the Joint Chiefs, "All hope of localization of the Korean conflict to enemy forces composed of North Korean troops with alien token elements can now be completely abandoned. The Chinese military forces are committed in North Korea in great and ever increasing strength. . . . We face an entirely new war."[10] MacArthur further added that UN forces did not have sufficient manpower to meet the new Chinese threat and that he had done everything humanly possible to keep the UN in the war. The Joint Chiefs informed MacArthur that they could not commit any more troops, nor did they want to even if they had the reserve. The United States still believed the North Korean invasion could be a diversion for an assault on Western Europe. And Japan had been stripped of much of its occupation force, leaving it exposed as well.

MacArthur recommended using the Nationalist troops offered by Chiang Kai-shek to reinforce faltering UN units and to launch diversionary attacks on the Chinese mainland. He also proposed a naval blockade of China's coast, air attacks on targets within China to cripple its war capability, and use of the atomic bomb. This, MacArthur claimed, was the only way he could hope to hold Korea. Otherwise, UN troops would have to be evacuated or face envelopment by the enemy. The Joint Chiefs and Washington considered MacArthur's proposals but found them to be too dangerous. Dean Acheson had stated to the UN that the Korean conflict had moved the United States closer to an all-out war, and any decision made at that point must be made with the knowledge that it could lead to war with the Soviet Union.

The Dismissal of MacArthur

MacArthur became increasingly vocal about the limits placed on his command. Since his recommendations through official channels were being dismissed, he turned to the press to express his concern. In an interview with the editors of *U.S. News & World Report*, MacArthur openly criticized Truman's limited war policy and called the restrictions placed on himself an "enormous handicap without precedent."[11] These statements not only discredited Truman's foreign policy, but they also threatened to undermine domestic and international support of the war, notably among U.S. allies. In response, Truman issued a directive to all executive personnel, though specifically aimed at MacArthur, that required all speeches and press releases be cleared with either the State or Defense Departments. The directive did curb MacArthur for a short period; but in March, during a period when Truman was proposing a cease-fire, MacArthur intentionally scuttled the peace process. President Truman had no choice but to relieve MacArthur of his command and appoint General Matthew Ridgway as his successor. This decision was made with the support of the Joint Chiefs and the executive staff. But it resulted in a heavy political and public backlash for Truman. America still considered MacArthur a hero.

Truman would be vindicated after the MacArthur hearings in 1951, but public opinion of the administration never improved. Public support for the war effort also continued to decline. MacArthur's dismissal and the entry of the Chinese into the war actually revived right-wing arguments about isolationism. Former president Herbert Hoover denounced on radio the high cost and futility of U.S. intervention. He advocated a withdrawal from Europe and Asia. He believed the United States should only be concerned with its own defense and become a self-sufficient entity, a "Gibraltar" protected by oceans and superior airpower. Although Hoover's ideas were extreme, they sparked the great debate about the proper role of the United States in the world. The debate continued throughout 1951 before being put to rest—though it would never disappear completely.

Ridgway Takes the Lead

General Matthew Ridgway was brought in at the end of 1950 to take command of the Eighth Army after his predecessor, General Walton Walker, had been killed in a Jeep accident. Ridgway could not keep Seoul from falling, but he was able to stop the UN's retreat. In short order, Ridgway was able to restore morale and make organizational changes that improved effectiveness of the Eighth Army. More importantly, Ridgway employed a new fighting strategy of slashing at the enemy with the intent to inflict maximum casualties as opposed to fighting for territory. He called it a war of maneuver, and it would take full advantage of the UN's artillery and airpower superiority. Throughout March 1951 these tactics proved deadly to Communist forces and resulted in a huge number of enemy casualties. UN forces were able to retake Seoul without a fight and cross the thirty-eighth parallel by the end of the month.

On April 11, 1951, Ridgway was given MacArthur's command of all UN forces. Ridgway turned over command of the Eighth Army to General James Van Fleet. Ridgway was initially skeptical of Van Fleet, but the general would quickly prove his worth. Van Fleet was welcomed into his new command by a massive Communist offensive aimed at reclaiming Seoul. The initial brunt of the assault forced UN troops to withdraw forty miles to avoid being enveloped by the enemy. The retreat, however, was an orderly one, and UN forces were able to regroup and repel the attacks. Van Fleet was eventually given permission to launch a new offensive. Unfortunately, many of the troops were battle weary, and the new program of rotating troops had sent a score of experienced veterans home. UN forces continued to advance, but at a slower pace.

By the end of May, the allies had shown the Communists that overwhelming numbers were not going to be enough to push them off the continent. At great cost to both sides, UN forces had reclaimed much of the ground they had lost during the spring offensives. And they established a strong defensive line close to where the war had been started. Van Fleet and other military leaders wanted to pursue the enemy, whose diminished morale and effectiveness were beginning to show. But Truman was under continuing pressure from the allies to make another tentative bid for peace. And he wanted to make it while the UN still had the upper hand. He dispatched George Kennan to discreetly discuss the matter with his Soviet contacts.

The Possibility of Peace

Acting as an intermediary, Jacob Malik, the Soviet delegate to the UN, broadly hinted over the radio that a peace settlement might be possible. After the Chinese and North Koreans endorsed Malik's proposal, Truman authorized Ridgway to contact his Communist counterpart and arrange a meeting. Both sides agreed to meet at the Communist-held town of Kaesong, south of the thirty-eighth parallel. Vice Admiral C. Turner Joy, commander of naval forces in the Far East, was chosen by Ridgway to conduct the negotiations on behalf of the UN. The chief delegates for the Communists were NKPA lieutenant general Nam Il and the vice premier of the Communist regime.

The talks began inauspiciously in an atmosphere of mistrust and hostility. It took two weeks to create an agenda of issues that needed to be resolved. Then, on August 23, the Communists broke off negotiations entirely because of an alleged UN violation of the cease-fire zone that surrounded Kaesong. The allies believed the Communists were intentionally delaying the negotiations so they could build up their forces and thus gain a better negotiating position. On the battlefield, the fighting continued uninterrupted since both sides had agreed at the outset that there would be no cease-fire until the armistice was signed. The United States had achieved some victories, but the war eventually slowed down. Both armies dug in and fought the same static line battles that had been fought during World War I.

The peace talks resumed in October and moved to the tiny settlement of Panmunjom. Negotiations were more productive the second time and resulted in the settlement of most of the problems that had been set by the agenda. There would, however, be two issues that would hang up the peace process for two years. The first issue involved the location of the demarcation line, which would establish the new border between North and South Korea. The United States wanted the border to rest on the current battle line, which was north of the thirty-eighth parallel. The Communists wanted the thirty-eighth parallel restored. They also wanted Kaesong. After five months of negotiation, the Communists finally agreed to give up the thirty-eighth parallel as long as they kept Kaesong. Washington conceded, against the vehement protests of Ridgway. Ridgway believed Kaesong had too much strategic value to give up despite the fact it resided behind enemy lines.

The second issue regarded POW repatriation. The Communists insisted the United States abide by the Geneva Convention of 1949, which specified the immediate return of all prisoners of war. The problem was that fifty thousand of the POWs did not want to return home. A large number of the Chinese POWs were former Nationalists who had fought against the Communists during the Chinese civil war. And many of the North Koreans just did not like Communist rule. The United States tried to negotiate for voluntary repatriation, but the Communists rejected the compromise. They considered acceptance to be an admission that they had failed to secure the loyalty of all of their citizens. Truman also chose to be inflexible on the matter. He considered forced repatriation a moral issue that was nonnegotiable.

Deadlocked

The negotiations were completely deadlocked in May 1952 and were further complicated by an uprising in a prison camp on Kojedo Island. The incident resulted in the camp commander, Brigadier General Francis Dodd, being held hostage. He was eventually released, but not before he signed a statement that validated the Communists' accusations that the UN had mistreated its POWs. The incident was later found to have been orchestrated by the Communist high command in an attempt to discredit the United States. It did not change the U.S. position, but it did raise worldwide concern. It was one of many issues that the Communists would take advantage of to try and better their bargaining position.

General Mark Clark, who had succeeded Ridgway as commander of UN forces, wanted to force the Communists to come to terms by turning up the bombing campaign. Nonmilitary targets such as Pyongyang and the North Korean hydroelectric plants on the Yalu were chosen. Unfortunately, the bombing campaign did not help at all, and, if anything, it just made the Communists more intractable.

In November 1952, Dwight D. Eisenhower became the

new president of the United States. One of his key campaign promises that helped him win the election was a quick end to the Korean War. In December he flew to Korea to fulfill his promise. General Clark submitted a comprehensive plan to Eisenhower on how to achieve victory. Clark proposed large-scale amphibious landings in North Korea and an extension of MacArthur's plans to assault bases in China. But just like Truman, Eisenhower was not interested in expanding the war and instead sought a political resolution.

Peace at Last

The truce talks were resumed in April 1953 after Stalin's death. Stalin's successor, Georgy M. Malenkov, one of Stalin's former aids, was more conciliatory and publicly stated that the Soviet Union and United States could settle disputes peacefully. The Communists agreed to a revised repatriation compromise, which allowed POWs who did not want to return to live in a neutral country. The treaty was signed on June 27, 1953. The United States, China, and North Korea signed the armistice agreement. South Korean president Syngman Rhee had been opposed to any kind of negotiations from the beginning and refused to sign, which has officially left the two Koreas still at war today.

Aftermath

Though the conflict between the two nations remained unresolved, all foreign troops were completely withdrawn from Korea. The two Koreas remained politically and ideologically divided and hostile toward each other. The final dividing line was so close to the original that neither side seemed to gain anything from the war except a massive list of casualties, widespread destruction, and some exploitable propaganda. North Korea and China claimed victory and earned a measure of world respect for matching the military might of the United States. The United States and the Soviet Union ended up embarking on a costly arms race that not only raised tensions between the two superpowers but also led them to the brink of war on several occasions. These tensions also led the United States down a familiar path with its participation in Vietnam, another Asian war that would end inconclusively.

Today, North Korea remains one of the world's last bastions of communism. It is still governed by the same regime that had existed since the Korean War. And though the Cold War has ended, North Korea retains its hard-line Communist traditions. The nation maintains a large military despite the economic hardships being experienced by its people. But reunification talks between the two nations continue and remain hopeful.

Notes

1. Bevin Alexander, *Korea: The First War We Lost*. New York: Hippocrene Books, 1986, p. 42.
2. Quoted in Burton I. Kaufman, *The Korean Conflict*. Westport, CT: Greenwood, 1999, p. 13.
3. Robert Kelley, *The Shaping of the American Past; vol. 2, 1865 to Present*, 5th ed. Englewood Cliffs, NJ: Prentice Hall, 1977, p. 817.
4. Quoted in Martin Walker, *The Cold War: A History*. New York: Henry Holt, 1993, p. 14.
5. Omar N. Bradley and Clay Blair, *A General's Life*. New York: Simon and Schuster, 1983, p. 476.
6. Charles E. Bohlen, *Witness to History: 1929–1969*. New York: W.W. Norton, 1973, p. 294.
7. Quoted in Alexander, *Korea*, p. 230.
8. David Rees, *Korea: The Limited War*. New York: St. Martin's, 1964, p. 100.
9. Quoted in Alexander, *Korea*, p. 258.
10. Quoted in Bradley and Blair, *A General's Life*, p. 598.
11. *U.S. News & World Report*, December 8, 1950, pp. 16–22.

1

WHAT'S AT STAKE IN KOREA

North Korea Is Another Step in the USSR's Plan of World Domination

Joseph Alsop and Stewart Alsop

The Alsop brothers, Joseph and Stewart, were the most widely read syndicated columnists of the 1950s and were known for their cynical viewpoints and their political predictions. The Alsop brothers accurately predicted such events as the Communist takeover in Czechoslovakia and the war in Korea, but they inaccurately predicted that the United States would enter a war with the Soviet Union in 1952 and that Harry Truman would be defeated by Thomas Dewey in the presidential elections of 1948.

In the following commentary, which appeared in the *Saturday Evening Post* in September 1950, the Alsops suggest that Communist North Korea's invasion of South Korea is another step in the USSR's plan for world domination. Many Alsop commentaries were unabashedly anti-Soviet, and this call to arms (written three months after the North Korean invasion) was no exception.

The lesson of Korea is grimly simple. Despite innumerable warnings, we did not do enough to deter Soviet aggression or to contain Soviet imperialism. Since the end of the Second World War, we have been on public notice from such authorities as [American diplomat and historian] George F. Kennan that any "soft spot" would tempt the Kremlin to attack. Only a few months ago, Secretary of State Dean G. Acheson told the Congress and the country that the Krem-

Joseph Alsop and Stewart Alsop, "The Lesson of Korea," *Saturday Evening Post*, September 2, 1950, pp. 17–19, 96, 98, 100. Copyright © 1950 by *Saturday Evening Post*. Reproduced by permission.

lin [Soviet Union] would seize any territory that was "within it grasp and reach."

Korea was a soft spot, within the Kremlin's grasp and reach. The strength of the West, and particularly the armed strength of the United States, was too slight to instill in the masters of the Kremlin any healthy fear of reprisals. Hence Korea was attacked.

Such are the obvious, surface facts. Beneath the surface, however, lies another set of facts of infinitely greater significance to every American. Korea is only the first episode of an attempt to bring all Asia and all Europe within the Soviet Empire. The Kremlin's true aim is not merely to seize the rocky hills of South Korea. It is not merely to grab anything that is not nailed down. The real Kremlin goal is to make the living death of the slave society the universal condition of mankind, from the shores of the Atlantic to the islands of Japan, from the icy cliffs of Spitsbergen [a group of islands in the Arctic Ocean, midway between Norway and the North Pole] to the bright sands of Cape Comorin [located at the southernmost tip of the Indian subcontinent].

The Kremlin's World Strategy

Furthermore, expert observers have already discerned the outlines of the well-conceived world strategy by which the masters of the Kremlin expect to reach their staggering goal. The existence of this Kremlin world strategy is solidly testified to by much other evidence than the Korean affair.

Indeed, there are good reasons to believe that the Soviet planners formally communicated the first part of their program to trusted Asiatic communist leaders at a secret conference in Peking nearly nine months ago. This meeting, held under the cover name of the "Asian and Australasian Bureau of the World Federation of Trades Unions," examined in detail the whole military-political situation in Asia and approved a policy of aggression on almost every front. It was then that Korea was probably tentatively chosen as the first point of attack.

Korea was chosen, in turn, precisely because it was a territory under American protection. This may be paradoxical. Yet it is the key to the whole problem. In brief, for excellent reasons which will be examined later, the Soviet planners expected no American response to the Korean attack. They hoped, therefore, for a rapid triumph, which would simultaneously show the great strength of the Soviet Union and expose the feebleness of the United States. And this, of course, is precisely the tactic on which the whole Kremlin world strategy is based. Two thirds of the world is to be conquered, not by overt onslaughts of the Red Army, but by carefully prepared, strictly localized, yet violently terrifying demonstrations of unchallengeable Soviet power.

How this can be is hard for most Americans to understand, in this rich, never-conquered, ocean-girdled, self-confident land. Yet the fact remains. In the blood-drained, neurotic world of the bad time after the second great war, brute strength can win battles where no blow is struck.

A Chain of Defeat to Start in Korea

We should soon have seen the truth of this if the Korean attack had turned out as the Kremlin intended. In Asiatic politics, the desire to back the winner always predominates. Such poor governments as that of [Elpidio] Quirino, in the Philippines, or the odd little gaggle of Socialist idealists who preside over the nation-wide riot in Burma, or the distracted administration of Sukarno and Hatta, in Indonesia, are neither deeply rooted nor powerfully led. The spectacle of a Kremlin triumph in Korea would have deeply intimidated the leaders of every new government in Asia. Their whole orientation would have been altered. And so the rot would have begun.

There is a reliable intelligence, moreover, that even as the Kremlin gave the order to march in Korea [North Korean premiere Kim Il Sung came to the decision on his own and launched his attack with the begrudging approval of the Soviet Union], plans had already been laid for a second, even more devastating attack on the great soft spot of the Middle East, oil-rich Iran. The subjugation of Iran—a combined operation of the "Azerbaijanian" divisions now training in Russia and the communist-front Tudeh Party within the borders—was projected for . . . autumn [1950]. A success in Iran would two thirds complete the collapse of Asia under Soviet pressure.

We may hope that this Iranian project has been upset by our firm response to the Korean challenge. But we cannot be sure. The plain fact is that a sudden show of American firmness was the last thing the Kremlin anticipated. The effect may be to knock the Kremlin strategy galley west. But precisely because this danger is inherent in our firmness, the effect may also be to make the Kremlin speed up the whole tempo of its effort far beyond anything previously planned. Before the odds in favor of either of these results can be intelligently calculated, however, it is first necessary to grasp what may be called the Kremlin strategy's tactical pattern.

This pattern is clear. In Korea, the Kremlin meant to start something exactly like the rapid caving of a muddy riverbank under the furious gnawing of a flood. Surrender was to lead, by easy stages, to surrender. Victory in Korea was to be the prelude to victory everywhere. This was emphasized and re-emphasized in every analysis of the Korean attack by the State Department experts. And it was for this reason, and this reason only, that the President gave the order to fight for Korea, which the armed services held long ago to be militarily valueless. [General Douglas MacArthur and Secretary of State Dean Acheson had, on two separate occasions, excluded the Korean Peninsula from the U.S. Pacific defense perimeter.]

Nor was the fate of Asia the sole consideration in those two anxious days at Blair House before the President made up his mind. In the vast convulsion that the Kremlin is attempting to engineer, the capture of Asia is only a phase, whereas the engulfment of Europe is the final objective. The new Soviet Empire must include Europe's great industrial potential, to balance Asia's hungry man power and unexploited raw materials. Northern France and the Low

Countries, steel-rich Sweden, the busy Po Valley and the vital Ruhr—these are the grand prizes in the Kremlin game.

A Little Deterrence Goes a Long Way

In Europe, to be sure, we have already proved we can win a great contest with the Kremlin if we only try. The Marshall Plan [originally suggested by Secretary of State George C. Marshall, which encouraged European countries to work together after World War II] has promoted an astonishing European recovery. Economic betterment has begun to cure Europe's postwar neuroses and has begun to transform the nations across the Atlantic into powerful potential allies of the United States. Indeed, there is no doubt that the Kremlin adopted its new world strategy, a direct borrowing from Adolf Hitler, precisely because we had already defeated the first postwar campaign for Europe, which was conducted on classic Stalinist lines of revolutionary infiltration and politico-economic disruption.

Yet an American diplomat who watched developments in Paris, the European nerve center, has called the forty-eight hours before President Truman's Korean decision "the worst two days of my life." A man long trained to be sensitive to such things, he saw the politicians beginning to trim their sails a little. He saw the editors walking on eggs in their comment on Soviet aggression. He saw the rich men hurrying to the banks to send away their money, and the poor men sadly reading the headlines and resigning themselves to the worst. After the 1930's, the first sorry signs of submission and appeasement were only too familiar to his eyes.

A Replay of Nazi German Conquest

Remember the 1930's, and you will instantly comprehend what the Kremlin can achieve in Europe. In the 1930's, Hitler took the Rhineland and Austria, the Sudetenland and Czechoslovakia with no shot fired, by the same tactics of terror and power that the Kremlin has now borrowed. The method was to use power to beget terror, to beget appeasement. In the 1950's, Western Europe is far weaker than in the 1930's—immeasurably less well armed, still exhausted by the shock of war, still divided by communist infiltration. Meanwhile, the Kremlin plays the power-and-terror game upon a larger stage than Hitler ever dreamed of. Iran, Burma and Indo-China, Berlin, Vienna and Belgrade are the scenes where the might of the Soviet Union is to be proved and the feebleness of the West is to be shown. The effect in Europe, if countermeasures are not taken, will be utterly paralyzing. . . .

An All-Out Effort Is Needed

As for the second part of the lesson of Korea, it is as unpleasant as the first. If we treat the Korea war as an isolated antibandit operation, every basic cause of the Kremlin's aggression there will continue to operate with increasing force. Soviet war preparations will go forward with mounting effectiveness—for the British and American intelligences believe that the Kremlin has moved in Korea three full years before the climax of the Russian rearmament. Meanwhile, our own power, by the same token, will grow relatively less with every passing month. Soon or late, another vulnerable flank will be attacked; whether Iran or Burma, or Berlin or Yugoslavia, it hardly matters. Again the iron engine of the Kremlin world strategy will begin to operate. And when that happens we shall have reached the pass to which [English prime ministers Stanley] Baldwin and [Neville] Chamberlain brought Britain.

We shall have to choose between launching a war of desperation or surrendering in our turn, for let no one suppose it will not mean eventual destruction, in this age of the absolute weapons, to be isolated in our hemisphere with all the resources and all the peoples of all the rest of the world arrayed against us by the Kremlin's hard hand.

If we wish to avoid this future choice, we must face the facts and do something about them. We must rebuild the defenses of the West without an instant's delay. For the true basis of the Kremlin's world strategy is not the vulnerability of the exposed flanks, like Korea and Iran, although this vulnerability plays its part. The true basis of the Kremlin's world strategy, in fact, is the simple predominance of the naked military power of the Soviet Empire over the armed strength of the United States and the free world. The real "soft spot" that invited the Korean attack was not the weakness of the ineffectual Syngman Rhee [president of the Republic of Korea] *but our own weakness.* . . .

What We Must Do

What we do must be conditioned not only by the longer-range factors already described but also by the existing military situation. Here is where the Korean attack has, obviously, produced the most direct effects. For a long time the available forces of our major potential allies have been pretty completely tied down. Almost the whole French professional army has long been committed in Indo-China [today known as Vietnam], leaving little strength even for the German occupation, while Britain's forces are thoroughly engaged, either in Germany or on ordinary but essential empire duties, as in the Middle East or in the antiguerrilla campaign in Malaya. This was less alarming while the forces of America were not committed. But because of our previous disarmament, the Korean attack has now required the total commitment, on this distant and difficult terrain, of all the existing free strength of the United States.

In contrast, except for the occupation army in Eastern Germany—which is in the hardest combat training—no important Soviet forces are committed anywhere. The new satellite armies are certainly sufficient to keep the slave populations in order. The whole Red Army, with all its numerous supporting arms, stands today disengaged, unchallenged and ready to be used tomorrow, if the Kremlin chooses, at any one of the numerous sensitive and strategic points where the Soviets have already indicated aggressive intentions. And in this situation of deadly peril, we further know that the Kremlin has adopted a world strategy aimed to bring all Eurasia within the Soviet Empire—which will surely be the prelude to the establishment of a Stalinist One World.

Such is the debit side of the balance sheet, which is dark indeed. Perhaps the masters of the Kremlin may have yielded to the strong temptation of these facts; perhaps they will have struck again and again, even in the short interval before these words are printed. Meanwhile, the balance sheet's credit side also must be examined.

First, there is one element of American strength that is not as yet committed—the Strategic Air Force and the stock of atomic weapons. In these categories, the masters of the Kremlin still suffer from deficiencies, although they are working hard to overcome them. Moreover, although they are improving it rapidly, they have not as yet completed the air defense of their homeland. On the recent European trip of one of these reporters, a great British air leader remarked to him, "We may as well face it; there's going to be a very bad time, which we'll have to get through on nerve plus willingness to use atomic weapons if necessary." That time is now upon us.

Second, there is the incompleteness of Soviet war preparations. The effects of the unfinished state of Russian rearmament should not be overestimated; but they should not be ignored either. Besides the more obvious problems of atomic stocks and air defense, already mentioned, transport deficiencies, for example, must also be a powerful deterrent. In the present state of the East-West rail-and-road net, it is even hard to see how Russia could deploy in Western Europe the great armies that would be demanded by a general war.

Third—and this is the most important point of all—the men who should know best from long, firsthand experience, are convinced that a general war is the one thing [Soviet dictator Joseph] Stalin and the Politburo still boggle at. The outcome must test the verdict of the experts. But it must be said that the expert view is supported by the nature of the Kremlin world strategy, so elaborately and astutely calculated to secure the effects of a gigantic victory in war by mere local operations, terror tactics and menaces.

And it must be said also that the other arguments that the experts offer are equally convincing.

To trace these arguments in any detail would require a second report as long as this one. Suffice it to say that there are two main ones. The first concerns the instability of the slave base of the Soviet power pyramid. After the German attack on Russia, the Russian villages greeted the invaders with bread and salt. Russian men volunteered, literally in hundreds of thousands, to serve in German divisions. Indeed, there is a mass of evidence that Hitler might have used the Russians to beat Russia, if his folly of racism had not led him to proclaim the policy of scorched earth, which in turn stimulated and solidified the Russian resistance. And if this was the situation in the Soviet Union in 1941, what must be the conditions in the satellites today?

As for the second argument, it is founded on personal observation of Joseph Vissarionovich Stalin himself, by such men as [U.S. diplomats] W. Averell Harriman, Charles E. Bohlen and Harry L. Hopkins. To all of these, and to many other Americans and Englishmen who saw him in wartime, Stalin repeatedly confessed his bottomless respect for the American industrial potential, when it was mobilized. None of those who have heard him on this subject thinks that the dictator of the new Soviet Empire will wish to court a general war with a mobilized America, however glittering may be the promises of early triumph.

Here, of course, is the final, the conclusive, the quintessential part of Korea's grim lesson. We and the whole free world are in most dreadful danger because we, as leaders of the free world, have ignored the inherent menace of Soviet war preparation. We may hope that the existing deterrents may still operate, for a while, to prevent the further Soviet aggressions that could lead only to a third world war. But we must face the cruel fact that these deterrents will operate at all only if we show ourselves ready to fight Russia herself, if need be, in order to save the cause of freedom in the world. And we must face the further cruel fact that even if we show this willingness, the existing deterrents are, all of them, wasting assets, which will grow less and less effective as the Russian rearmament continues.

In this position to which our own folly has brought us, we have only one recourse. Everything that can conceivably contribute to the strength of the free world must now be done without hesitation, without question, without regard to politics or cost. Whether the need is to extend and improve our intelligence effort, or to set on foot a propaganda, by clandestine means if necessary, to defeat the Partisans of Peace, or to give massive aid to Yugoslavia or vastly to expand our military-aid program—it must be done.

Above all, the whole resources of this country and the whole available resources of our allies must now be mobilized fully and forthwith to rebuild with all speed a solid defense of the West. Even in the short time that is left to us, we can still hope to do the job if we go all out. But in this short time we cannot hope to rebuild the defenses of the West by the flaccid and comfortable methods of the pretended rearmament program that Stanley Baldwin offered Britain after the 1935 election. There will be comfort-loving, complacent souls who will plead for this; they must be dismissed with contempt.

Security for the free world cannot now be purchased cheaply. We must not only steel ourselves for a period of unnerving risks. We must also prepare for a period of heavy personal sacrifices. It is the only way. At least, it is the only way unless we prefer to indulge ourselves for a fugitive instant, and then to see the totalitarian silence and the night of the soul close over this world of ours.

America's Foreign Policy

John Foster Dulles

Many historians consider Secretary of State John Foster
Dulles to be the quintessential hard-liner. Dulles believed
communism to be a moral evil that had to be resisted at all
costs, and he advocated the buildup of atomic arms as a deterrent against Communist expansion and as a tactic in enemy attack. Dulles initially supported President Harry Truman's Cold War policy, which sought to prevent Soviet
expansion. But after Truman's dismissal of General Douglas MacArthur, Dulles joined with other Republicans to denounce Truman's containment policy, calling it "negative,
futile and immoral." The following speech was made before a foreign policy conference at Colgate University on
July 7, 1950.

The Korean affair obviously brings us nearer to the day of
fateful decision. Also, it makes it more probable that we
will make the kind of effort needed to fend off the utter disaster of war.

The danger of war has lain largely in our past failure to
see clearly and respond adequately to the peril that stems
from Soviet communism. That slowness is probably inevitable in a democracy when national policy depends on
public opinion. However, even now it is not too late to put
peace onto a more stable basis than ever before.

The nature of the Soviet Communist threat has been
fully set out by [Soviet dictator Joseph] Stalin himself in his
Problems of Leninism. The latest English edition, printed

John Foster Dulles, "U.S. Military Actions in Korea," *Department of the State
Bulletin,* July 3–December 25, 1950.

in Moscow, is dated 1940. Stalin there outlines the program, whereby, Soviet communism expects to extend its system throughout the world and establish its "one world" of state socialism. The plan is to conquer the weaker countries, one by one, by methods of propaganda, penetration, subversive warfare, and, as a last resort, open war. The strongest non-Communist countries, notably the United States, will be left to the last and, gradually, encircled and their economies weakened until, finally, they are supposed either to capitulate voluntarily or be overthrown by open assault which the Communist countries will presumably then have the power to launch successfully. Stalin points out, and this dates back to 1925, that the "road to victory" over the West lies through "revolutionary alliance with the liberation movement" in the colonies and countries of the East. The hostile tide of communism in Asia, which looms so dangerously today, has been announced and actively nurtured for 25 years.

Stalin's Strategy

Stalin's book, which is the present-day Communist bible, except in Yugoslavia, gives us the same preview that [Nazi leader Adolf] Hitler gave in *Mein Kampf*. There is, however, an important distinction between the Hitler program and the Stalin program. Hitler felt that his whole program had to be achieved in short order, during his own lifetime. That required intensive and sustained offensive action. In the case of the Communist program, there is no such time urgency. It is anticipated that full realization of the Communist conquest may take what Stalin refers to as "an entire historical era." And, he teaches, that "tactics of retreat" are as important as tactics of attack. Also, he teaches, the necessity of compromise when, as he puts it, this is necessary "to buy off a powerful enemy and gain a respite."

Therefore, under the Communist program, war by Russia is not necessarily inevitable or imminent if we are powerful enough to make it seem expedient to the Soviet Communist leaders to use tactics of delay or compromise.

The United States Awakens to Reality

We have only recently begun to take seriously Stalin's world program for communism, long announced, superbly implemented, and already one-third consummated. Our national attitude has only gradually moved toward realism. There has been an evolution through four phases:

1. *Cooperation*—That was the war phase. When Hitler made the Soviet Union and the United States war allies, there was a military necessity of cooperation that made it expedient to draw a veil over the basically hostile attitude of Soviet communism toward the United States. We emphasized the courageous fighting qualities of the Russian people, and we ignored the basic antipathy toward us of the Communist leaders. On the theory that the Soviet Union had to be given inducements to prevent her making a separate peace with Germany and to get her to enter into the war against Japan, we agreed to go along with large Soviet postwar expansion in both central Europe and in Asia.

2. *Noncooperation*—The second phase of our policy came immediately after the close of the fighting. The Soviet Union then sought to secure continuing support from the United States for her expansionist policy. Her leaders argued that postwar cooperation of the Soviet Union and the United States was necessary in order to assure world peace and that that cooperation necessitated the United States acquiescing in the expansionist ambitions of the Soviet Union. That was in essence the Molotov thesis which was presented [by Soviet diplomat Vyacheslav Molotov] at the first Council of Foreign Ministers meeting at London, in September 1945, which I attended with Secretary [of State James] Byrnes. We then made the momentous decision that we would not continue in time of peace the Yalta type of appeasement which had seemed necessary in time of war.

That decision taken at London, in the fall of 1945, did not, however, immediately make itself felt throughout all aspects of the United States foreign policy. Notably, there was a lag in bringing our Eastern policy into line with our Western policy. Many Eastern students were impressed by the abuses and deficiencies of existing Eastern governments and felt that a good dose of Communist reform might be healthy.

3. *Prevention*—The third phase of American policy was marked by realization that there was in fact an irreconcilable conflict between the ambitions of Soviet communism and the interests and welfare of the United States and that we needed to assert ourselves positively to prevent the extension of Soviet communism. This new approach came out of the 1947 Moscow and London Conferences of the Council of Foreign Ministers which I attended with Secretary [of State George C.] Marshall. Between these two Council meetings came the Marshall Plan proposal (June 1947). We then clearly saw that we were threatened by a so-called "cold war," and we made up our minds to make positive efforts to strengthen the free world and to fill up military, economic, and moral vacuums into which Soviet communism was moving.

Our maximum efforts were directed to Europe. But there was also a change of policy in the Far East, as indicated by the fact that in August 1948 Secretary Marshall advised our Embassy in China that "the United States Government must not directly or indirectly give any implication of support, encouragement, or acceptability of coalition government in China with Communist participation."

We have, however, up to now, assumed, and that was a fair working hypothesis, that communism would probably limit itself to "cold war" tactics and that there would not be open military attack. However, some preparations were made as against the possibility of armed attack, notably in Western Europe. We made the North Atlantic Treaty and adopted the Military Assistance Program.

4. *Opposition*—The fourth phase of policy is marked by the North Korean attack upon South Korea and our active fighting opposition under the direction of the United Nations. The Korean affair shows that communism cannot be checked merely by building up sound domestic economies. The South Korean experiment in democracy was as hopeful as could be expected. There was political, intellectual,

and economic freedom. The second national election had just been held, and the majority elected were independent of the party in power which controlled the police force and the election machinery. The fact that that could happen is good evidence of political freedom. As recently as 2 weeks ago, I met with the Korean National Assembly, with leading educators, with religious groups, businessmen, and representatives of labor. I conferred with our mission, and economic advisers, and with the Korean Commission of the United Nations. All the evidence was that the Republic of Korea provided a wholesome, free society and one which could not be overthrown by subversive efforts. Such efforts had, indeed, been repeatedly tried and had failed. The military blow from the north dissipates the thesis that internal reform and well-being is itself a sufficient defense against Communist aggression.

The Korea Attack Was Part of the Communist Plan

The armed attack that occurred shows that, while the Soviet Union seems not at the moment prepared to engage its own army, nevertheless, international communism is prepared to use, in open warfare, the armed forces of puppet and satellite Communist states which are equipped with armament of Russian manufacture.

It was realized for some time that the Republic of Korea was in danger of attack from the north. Proof of that is found in the fact that the United Nations continued its Korean Commission after the government of the Republic had been set up under United Nations supervision, and in the fall of 1949, the General Assembly added to the functions of the Commission the task of maintaining military observation along the northern frontier.

When, I, myself, went to the Far East, on June 14th, it was primarily to look into the possibilities of the Japanese peace treaty. But I went first to Korea to acquaint myself personally with a situation which, for several years, I had dealt with as a United States delegate to the United Nations. I was concerned about the increasing insistence by the North Korean Communist regime that it must rule all of Korea and the intensive Communist propaganda in South Korea that it had better succumb to communism without resistance, because neither the United Nations nor the United States would give protection if the Republic should be attacked.

Before leaving Washington, I drafted a speech to be made in Korea. In it I said that if the Republic of Korea were attacked, it could expect support from the United Nations. I pointed out that the United Nations Charter required all nations "to refrain from any threat or use of force against your territorial integrity or political independence" and, I added, that the United States stood behind the United Nations. I concluded with these words:

> You are not alone. You will never be alone so long as you continue to play worthily your part in the great design of human freedom.

That address was made on June 19th at the opening of the Second National Assembly. It was broadcast in the Korean language, throughout Korea, and Korean language leaflet copies were widely distributed. Nevertheless, 6 days later the North Korean army struck, in a long-prepared and fully implemented effort. There were ample supplies of Russian-made planes, tanks, and heavy artillery. The Republic's army fought bravely but hopelessly. It had no combat planes, no tanks, and no artillery heavy enough to stop the invading tanks. Unopposed enemy planes flew low, strafing the civilian population, setting fire to gasoline supplies, and spreading terror throughout the capital area. In 3 days, Seoul, 30 miles south of the northern border, was captured, and the tank formations moved on to the south.

A New Phase in American Foreign Policy

This open military attack and United Nations resistance to it opens a new phase in American foreign policy. It will, I hope and believe, arouse us to a greater effort than any we have yet made to fend off the danger of war. It may require us to devote a greater percentage of our vast economic productivity to military production so that other free nations will not be exposed to being overrun by Communist satellite forces equipped with armament furnished by Russia.

What has happened to the Republic of Korea shows, I fear, that the communistic assaults cannot be prevented merely by economic aid or merely by developing good societies. The open military assault on the Republic of Korea occurred because the Republic of Korea was too good a society to be tolerated on the otherwise Communist-dominated mainland of north Asia, and because it was so good that it could not be overthrown from within by indirect aggression. Direct aggression was the only way to blot out this moral salient on the Communist mainland.

There are probably two further reasons for the attack. One was that if it succeeded it would envelop Japan both from the north, where the Russians now have already gained hold of all of Sakhalin Island and the Kurile Islands, and from the south, where Korea is only separated by a narrow strait from the south of Japan. There was doubtless a desire to throw a roadblock in the way of the positive program of the United States for putting Japan onto a peaceful and self-governing basis, as part of the free world.

Furthermore, the Communists doubtless calculated that if the attack failed through the use of United States force to repel the attack, the process would bog down the West in the mire of anticolonialism in Asia.

As we have seen, Stalin long ago calculated that the best way to conquer the West was to involve it in fighting the anticolonial aspirations of Asia and the Pacific. The colonial powers, including the United States in the Philippines, Britain in India, Burma, and Ceylon, and the Dutch in Indonesia, by wise statesmanship, extricated themselves largely from this trap. No doubt the Korean venture is designed in part to draw the Western world back into that trap. That is a danger that has to be carefully avoided by relating our conduct to the policies of the United Nations which, as an organization, is strongly dedicated to self-government and independence for the non-self-governing peoples of the world.

Prospects for Peace

The situation is certainly fraught with danger.

However, if the members of the United Nations support and make good the Security Council decision to repel and throw back the unprovoked military aggression in Korea; if the defensive military position around the periphery of Soviet control is strengthened, so that satellite forces cannot easily break through with violence; if the colonial powers support the newly born nations and avoid general entanglement with the legitimate independence aspirations of the Asiatic peoples; then there will be a condition where peace is likely, unless the Soviet Union itself commits its total might to total war. It may not be prepared to do this because of its relative economic weakness.

Speaking in Tokyo on June 23, 1950, I pointed out that, in terms of key commodities such as steel, aluminum, electric power, and crude oil, the United States had an advantage over the Soviet Union of anywhere from five or ten to one. I concluded "Any struggle that openly pitted the full might of the free world against that of the captive world could have but one outcome. That would be the total demolition of the artificial, rigid, and relatively weak structure that Soviet communism has built." I believe that that is a correct analysis of the present situation. I do believe, however, that it will be necessary for us to convert more of our economic potential into present strength in order that the free nations who are menaced by Communist military attack can be better protected.

In the case of Korea, it was felt necessary to give a very low priority to the military position of the Republic of Korea because of the great shortage of available military equipment. Congress had appropriated funds to extend the Military Assistance Program to Korea. However, it had not yet been found possible to convert that appropriation into a reality. When I was there, the Korean defense establishment pointed out that while the morale and discipline of the Republic's army was first class, they could not be expected to hold for long without a single combat plane, without any tanks, without antiaircraft guns, and without artillery sufficient to stop the known concentrations of enemy tanks on the border.

We are now having to make good that deficiency in a costly way.

What has happened in Korea will, I think, bring home to the American people the need of adequate measures to strengthen the free world as against the possibility of sudden, armed attack. If we do that, we can close the most dangerous remaining loophole for war.

If we have strength; if we and the other members of the free world put that strength at the disposition of the United Nations; if the United Nations continues to show a capacity for decisive action, that will check the likelihood of a series of little wars which could develop into a big war.

Relations between the free world and the Communist world are no doubt in a dangerous phase. It is a period of testing. Out of it could come great disaster. Equally, the test could supply proof that peace has been established on a basis sounder than ever before in history.

The Korean War Was Not a Prelude to a Global Conflict

Charles E. Bohlen

Many of Truman's staff, including hawkish secretary of state Dean Acheson, believed that the Korean War was a prelude to a bigger conflict. U.S. diplomat and noted expert on Soviet affairs Charles E. Bohlen opposed this theory from the beginning. He believed the conflict was restricted to Korea, and he states in his autobiography that the Soviet Union just was not ready for an all-out war against the United States. Though Bohlen supported repelling the North Korean attack, he opposed launching a counterattack across the thirty-eighth parallel. He and a minority of other analysts rightfully surmised that Allied troops near the Chinese border would force the Chinese, and possibly the Soviet Union, into the war. Unfortunately, they were correct. And because of this miscalculation, the war was prolonged when the Chinese entered into the conflict.

On June 25, 1950, my wife and I were in our weekend cottage in Thiers, north of Paris. About lunchtime, I received a call from Woodruff Wallner, a Secretary in the Embassy, who told me that fighting had broken out in Korea. He motored out, bringing me the latest dispatches, and we returned together that afternoon. The following day, Ambassador [David] Bruce, Averell Harriman, who was then coordinator of the Marshall Plan [the postwar U.S. program that offered aid and assistance to war-ravaged European countries vulnerable to Communist influence], and I discussed the situation. We were relatively gloomy, because we saw no sign that the United States intended to take any vigorous action to stop the Communist invasion of South Korea. We speculated on the consequences of American inaction, how disheartening it would be to our allies, and how much danger it posed for the future. While we were sitting there, a cable from President [Harry] Truman arrived. It reported his decision to intervene with air and sea forces, and instructed Bruce to inform the French government. I accompanied Bruce when he called on Robert Schuman, the French Foreign Minister. Schuman's eyes filled with tears. "Thank God," he said, "this will not be a repetition of the past." He was thinking of the French and British failures to stop Hitler before World War II.

After a telephone conversation with Washington, it was decided that I would accompany Harriman back to Washington. We went to London to catch a plane. I remember the ride well. We wondered what was going to happen in Korea. Everything was uncertain, and the bumpy plane ride symbolized our emotions. . . .

We Were in the Minority

At [Secretary of State Dean] Acheson's request, I spent a month in Washington examining evidence to ascertain whether the Korean invasion was the forerunner of similar Communist military moves elsewhere in the world. I was working then with Gustav Hilger, whom I had known when he was German Minister in Moscow during the early years of the war and who happened to be in Washington. He was called in as a consultant after Korea. Born in Russia, he was fluent in the Russian language and an acknowledged expert on Soviet affairs. My conclusion was that there was little chance of the Soviet Union's repeating the invasion in any other place, such as Germany. The Soviet action in Korea was limited strictly to Korea.

Hilger and [American diplomat George] Kennan shared my view, but we were in the minority. The Korean war was interpreted by Acheson and most others in the State Department, as well as the Joint Chiefs of Staff, as ushering in a new phase of Soviet foreign policy. Their view, which Truman accepted, was that having launched an attack on Korea—the first case of Communist open use of naked military force to expand the system—the Soviet Union was likely to call on satellite armies elsewhere, particularly in East Germany, to spread Communist control. They were understandably influenced by the emotions engendered by the Communist invasion. At various meetings, Kennan and I argued in vain against this thesis.

We were particularly opposed to plans for a counterinvasion of North Korea. We warned that Communist countries would react strongly if hostile forces approached their borders. We had both China and the Soviet Union in mind, of course. Basic to our thinking was our conviction that the main objective of the leaders of Communist countries is preservation of the system. American troops on the Chinese border at the Yalu River, only a short distance from Vladivostok, would certainly be viewed as a threat. It was folly, Kennan and I argued, to take the chance of prodding China and/or the Soviet Union into a war. Sufficient military force should be used to throw back the invaders, we agreed, but large-scale retaliation was not necessary because the attack on Korea was not a prelude to invasions elsewhere.

Why were we so sure in the face of opposing opinions? In the first place, the Soviet Union was far from ready, from a strategic military point of view, to contemplate a global war with the United States. It had been less than a year since the Soviet Union exploded its first atomic bomb. While the test was earlier than many expected, we knew from our experience that the gap between the production of the first device and a usable arsenal of weapons was years. In June, 1950, it was beyond the realm of possibility that the Soviet Union had a stockpile of atomic weapons.

I believe that [Soviet leader Joseph] Stalin's chief motive was the desire to round out his hold over the entire Korean peninsula. By 1950, he realized that there was practically no chance of repeating in Japan his success in carving out a section of Germany. The refusal of the United States through Harriman to accord Stalin an occupational zone on the island of Hokkaido and [General Douglas] MacArthur's one-man rule made that clear. In addition, the United States was pushing ahead with plans for a peace treaty with Japan, and the Soviets were powerless to hold it up. But South Korea, practically defenseless since American forces had withdrawn, looked available for the taking.

Stalin also believed he could get away with the invasion because of his continued adherence to a classic error of Marxist thought, that the working class and poor were with the Communists everywhere. Not learning from his disappointment in Finland, he banked on the shock of the invasion to trigger off an internal revolt against the capitalist regime of President Syngman Rhee. While it is true that South Korea had no large working class, the Bolsheviks believed the poor peasants would on the whole favor a Communist regime. This fallacy cannot be avoided by a genuine Marxist-Leninist, for abandonment of this tenet would result in the collapse of the whole attempt to make Bolshevik theory applicable to all countries at all times. There was little doubt that Stalin and the North Korean dictator, Kim Il Sung, believed that the military action would be quick, with the South Koreans rising to support the Communists, and there would be no chance for any other country to do anything.

I am not one of those who believe that Acheson's speech to the National Press Club on January 12, 1950, in which he left Korea outside the limits of American vital interest in the Far East, had anything to do with the Soviet determination to approve, if not actually order, the attack on South Korea. It is difficult to imagine that a ruler as careful as Stalin would act on the basis of a speech to the press. His experience and instinct were to reject public statements as not necessarily defining a country's real position. It is probably true that Stalin did weigh the speech in the light of the total withdrawal of American military support from South

Korea and came to the conclusion that the United States would not act, especially if the invasion quickly took over the whole country. It was certainly not the speech itself that triggered any Soviet action.

The Soviet Union Was Directly Involved

There are those who now say that the war was not started by the Soviet Union but by an independent act of the North Koreans. This is childish nonsense. How could an army, trained in every respect by the Soviet Union, with Soviet advisers at every level, and utterly dependent on Moscow for supplies, move without Soviet authorization? Stalin would not have been so careless as to permit the North Koreans to kick off a war that conceivably might involve the Soviet Union in a confrontation with the United States. The Soviet Union has never joked about war.

Back in Paris, I was happy to read of General Douglas MacArthur's successful landing at Inchon, but I continued to be worried about the entry of Chinese or Russian forces. On November 25, three days after American troops reached the Yalu, Chinese "volunteers" crossed the river in overwhelming numbers. . . .

While Kennan and I were correct in our prediction about Chinese intervention, I do not know even now whether Stalin would have stood by and swallowed a total American victory in Korea. I believe Stalin never dreamed the United States would intervene. He thought the attack would be viewed as simply part of a civil war. Once the United States responded and the battle began to go against the Communist forces, I believe Stalin began to fear that the Soviet Union might be pulled into a big war. When the Chinese "volunteers" pushed the Americans back, Stalin must have been worried that the United States would use greater force, perhaps atomic weapons. He looked around for a way to extricate himself from the predicament he had got into. He certainly did not want to tangle with the American giant by launching other invasions.

Whether Stalin was instrumental in getting the Chinese to

enter the war is buried in the Moscow and Peking archives. It may well be that the Chinese dictator, Mao Tse-tung, decided on his own to intervene, because the threat to the Chinese Communist regime was too great for it to stand by. The Soviets were certainly perfectly willing to have the Chinese sacrifice their blood to defend North Korea. . . .

In September [1951], I was invited by General Omar Bradley, then chairman of the Joint Chiefs of Staff, to accompany him on an inspection tour of the front. Somewhat bored by my regular duties, I jumped at the chance, and we took off for Tokyo, flying via the Aleutian Islands. In Tokyo, we were briefed by General Matthew Ridgway, who had been appointed Supreme Commander in the Far East after General MacArthur was dismissed by Truman. I remember that Ridgway told General Bradley that if we were to contemplate winning a military victory in Korea at that stage, he would need six or seven more American divisions. With the war so unpopular in the United States, that was an impossibility.

We flew to Seoul, where we spent the night. There I found an old friend, Alan Lightner, who was political adviser to the American armies in Korea. He filled me in on the political situation. Bradley and I visited the front, from one side to the other, and I was awed by the ruggedness of the terrain. . . .

After four days in Korea, we flew back to Japan for more briefings. General Ridgway had stabilized the front, driving the enemy back so that the lines were roughly where they had been when the war started. Ridgway gave the impression of being and exceedingly competent military officer who knew his business down to the ground and who had clear, simple, and direct ideas on how things should be done. He did not bother too much about the nuances of international and diplomatic relations. . . .

The next morning, we flew to Anchorage, Alaska, through the mist and fog of the Aleutians. When we landed, the weather had cleared and we were treated to the full splendor of an Alaskan autumn day. We lunched at the officers' mess at the air base there, and Bradley conferred with the commander. Then we took off for the nonstop flight to Washington.

Although I personally profited from my first really close observation of warfare and I had certainly learned more about the reality of the Korean situation, nothing of great value emerged from General Bradley's trip. He informed General Ridgway that the United States had no intention of increasing the number of divisions in Korea, because at least partial mobilization would have been required. Bradley's visit did confirm the prevailing opinion in Washington that there was little hope of a military victory. . . .

Truman Helped Stop Communism in Its Tracks

When all is said about Korea, however, the fact remains that the two men responsible for finally blocking the expansion of Communism there were the cocky little President of the United States, Harry S Truman, and his icy-eyed Secretary of State, Dean Acheson.

Harry Truman did a superb job as President. Like everyone else, I felt considerable concern when he unexpectedly became President. He had no background in foreign affairs. He knew almost nothing of the arrangements that [President Franklin] Roosevelt had made with [English prime minister Winston] Churchill or Stalin or the details of the wartime conferences at Teheran and Yalta. Roosevelt apparently never conceived of the possibility that he might die in office. In contrast with Roosevelt, Truman studied the files and the papers prepared for him and was well prepared on all aspects of a subject when the time came for discussion and decision-making. He had one of the most important qualities necessary to be an effective president, a genuine power of decision. He lived up to the sign on his desk, "The buck stops here." Occasionally, his decisions would be too quick, but he was not hasty in foreign affairs. . . .

Like all of us, Truman was a creature of his times. To deal with the postwar problems required great decisions. It was impossible in the circumstances of 1945–52 to handle foreign affairs in a haphazard or superficial manner. Many of the problems he faced required "put up or shut up" answers. His firmness with [French president Charles] de Gaulle, which led the French to back down in their use of force to gain north Italian areas, and with [Yugoslav leader Josip] Tito over Trieste; his leadership of the European economic recovery; his support of Greece and Turkey; his courage and carefulness in the Berlin blockade; and his decision to use American armed force in Korea—none of these decisions could have been made by a second-rate president. Truman measured up to the demands thrust upon him.

It remains an incontestable fact that the major foundations of American foreign policy for decades were adopted during Truman's administration. The Greek-Turkish action set the pattern for our assistance to other governments beset by subversion supported from the outside; the Marshall Plan was the forerunner of all of the aid programs, and NATO [North Atlantic Treaty Organization] remains one of the cornerstones of our foreign policy.

Dean Acheson: Truman's Top Adviser
Truman relied heavily on his assistants, and extended to them the same degree of loyalty that he demanded from them. In the early days of his administration, he tended to place confidence only in some old friends, whom he brought into the White House. Some of these men were not up to the job. Since they had little effect on foreign affairs, there is no need for me to name them. His chief adviser, following the departure of General Marshall in the beginning of 1949, was Dean Acheson. Because I was out of the country for at least 50 percent of Truman's presidency, I could not estimate the influence of his other advisers. One thing is certain; they all relied heavily on Acheson, who had worked out an admirable relationship with the President. The Secretary of State came up with many of the ideas; the President, and the President alone, made the decisions. . . .

While he was a good Secretary of State at a critical point

in history, I do think he was wrong in some important historical judgments, particularly about Korea. I have already mentioned that Kennan and I concluded that Stalin's intention in Korea was simply to get control of the whole country, largely because he realized that there was very little chance of his playing the same type of sabotage role in Japan that he had played in Germany. Acheson, influenced, I think, by those in the State Department who did not know Soviet Russia, felt that the Korean war represented a new Soviet foreign policy of military expansion and that all of the areas contiguous to the free nations in Europe were threatened by attack.

As the result of this erroneous judgment, the United States overinterpreted the Korean war and overextended our commitments. The government concluded that godless Communism had conspired to take over the world and that the United States was the knight in shining armor who would fight it everywhere. Before Korea, the United States had only one commitment of a political or military nature outside the Western Hemisphere. This was the North Atlantic Treaty. Our bases in Germany and Japan were regarded as temporary, to be given up when the occupation ended. True, as a hangover from prewar days, we felt it necessary to retain bases in the Philippines, but there was no pledge on their use. The only other places we had military facilities were in England, where we had transit privileges, and Saudi Arabia, where we had an airfield. As a result of our overinterpretation of Communism's goal, we had by 1955 about 450 bases in thirty-six countries, and we were linked by political and military pacts with some twenty countries outside of Latin America. It was the Korean war and not World War II that made us a world military-political power.

Russian World Domination Is a Myth

James Samuel Stemons

The common perception during the 1950s is that America's entry into the Korean War was necessary to combat the USSR and its plan for world domination. But author James Samuel Stemons believes the Soviet Union is not directly responsible for the invasion (and recent evidence shows that he was correct). According to Stemons, the justification for settling matters through warfare is based on faulty presumptions that will only lead to America's own downfall. Stemons states that the war could have been prevented or at least the bloodshed limited and the war quickly ended if the North Koreans, South Koreans, the United States, and the USSR are truly willing.

Instead of the horrors, brutalities, hatreds, and devastations of war, the only sane and logical antidotes for communism are social and economic conditions which are far more inviting than anything which that nightmare has to offer. Social conditions are controlled largely by mass attitudes. Economic conditions are largely matters of industrial policies and unhampered opportunities. Social conditions aside, there are well-defined ways in which a minute fraction of the hundreds of billions which have been expended, and are still being expended by America in fantastic efforts to contain communism by shot and shell could, instead of pauperizing this nation and inviting social disruption, be so applied, right here in America, to say nothing about the universe, as to completely eradicate that nostrum from the human equation.

Adverting to our rash and incessant threats to atom-bomb Russia in the event of any more insular ructions: Passing over the obvious fact that such threats are direct provocatives for Russia to do the first bombing, as an elemental step toward self-preservation, those who are capable of doing their own thinking will doubtless be curious to know just why it is so essential for America to become embroiled in every conceivable insular flare-up while Russia, with seemingly just as much at stake, does little more than twiddle her thumbs—and look the other way. So far as the United Nations and Korea are concerned, many earnest persons feel that its functions have been gravely perverted and discredited by the aggressively partisan and disruptive part it has been forced to play.

One of the most significant aspects of these insular ructions is the fact that the factions favorable to Russia almost invariably do at least most of their own fighting, while the factions aligned with America leave their fighting to be done largely, if not solely by the Americans. The popular explanation for this anomalous situation is that Russia wins fanatical support from its *puppets* and *stooges* chiefly through unconscionable lies and slanders against the United States, as well as by grossly falsifying the actual principles and policies of communism. It would be uncandid to deny that Russia does slander and misrepresent the United States as well, perhaps, as make false claims for communism. Americans will be merely deluding themselves, however, and inviting dire consequences for the future, by ignoring the fact that Russia's tremendous hold upon hundreds of millions of human beings stems from much deeper roots than can be traced to any form of slander or misrepresentation. . . .

Events Came to Their Own Head

There seems to be even more impressive evidence that Russia in no way favored any such crazy turn of affairs as was represented by that Korean upheaval. No other argument seems essential to this proposition than that, in the very nature of things, it blew sky high the plans which were then well under way for the admission of Communist China to the United Nations, one of Russia's long cherished and perhaps most ardent dreams. In fact, there seems to be much evidence that the Korean upheaval climaxed an ideological conflict (made possible by nothing except the arbitrary cleavage of Korea by America and Russia) which had been raging for months between North and South Korea. In a release from Hong Kong on June 26, William R. Moore ("For more than two years Associated Press Correspondent in South Korea") said:

"Two bad setbacks this year may have goaded the Communist regime in North Korea into springing its long-threatened invasion of South Korea at this time. . . . The Red regime had sworn almost daily for the last two years to destroy the Southern Government, which it labels as a pawn of 'American imperialism.' The favorite Communist weapons—guerilla and underground political activity—both have proved failures. Another weapon the North counted on was time. Unexpectedly, it seemed to be favoring rather than harming the growth of democracy in the South. The Reds were left with only one weapon: Open war.

"For two years I watched these rival regimes develop, the North in what had been the Russian occupation zone, the South in the former American occupation zone. After the absence of only 10 weeks from Korea, I was surprised that the North had chosen to use armed force at this time. The status quo seemed to be profitable for Russia, which calls the tune for North Korea. Most reliable information reaching Seoul was that Russia was successfully exploiting North Korea economically, taking out a big share of the products of its factories and forests. It also seemed likely that Russia would find North Korea useful as an insulation belt between Manchuria—where the Soviets reportedly hope for exploitation—and South Korea, last outpost of the anti-Communist world. . . .

"Despite charges by the South Koreans, Chinese Nationalists, and others that the present invasion is an open act of Soviet aggression, it appears logical to expect Russia to foster the appearance that this is nothing but a purely Korean civil war—even at the risk of having all Korea move into the democratic camp. It is well to remember that the optimistic South Koreans frequently have threatened, 'if the Communists ever try to invade our territory, we'll chase them back to the Manchurian border. . . .'"

Of course these various weighty conclusions may not set well with those who are whipping America into a frenzy of fear and fury over a purely fictional charge that this Korean eruption represents nothing but a deliberate scheme by Russia to subdue and dominate the world by armed aggression. However, we have reached a point in human history where it may easily become disastrous for men to be swayed by vague suspicions and hysteria, rather than by the ascertainable facts as revealed by sober, competent, and impartial students and investigators. . . .

China Gets Involved

Most unfortunately, the latest decision of our State Department in connection with that Korean muddle precipitated a stalemate which killed every conceivable hope for a negotiated, conclusive, or satisfactory peace. Here are some of the more conspicuous developments incident to that alarming blunder:

Late in September, the United Nations forces began to drive the North Koreans toward the 38th Parallel. Fear immediately developed at Lake Success [UN headquarters in Rhode Island] that pursuit of the North Koreans beyond the 38th Parallel might cause a disastrous spread of the conflict. In fact, on October 5, Chou En-lai, Foreign Minister of the People's Republic of China, warned that China would not stand idly by "if the 38th Parallel is crossed."

The United States then began a contention, which was echoed by some of her Allies, that Chou En-lai was only bluffing and would not dare to attack the United Nations forces. However all this may have been, for the apparent purpose of playing safe, the South Koreans alone were assigned the risk of pursuing the North Koreans across the 38th Parallel. To the surprise and consternation of the United Nations forces, the North Koreans promptly hurled them back in wild confusion. Apparently nettled by this sudden reversal and humiliation, General [Douglas] MacArthur (though he has since insisted that he was following orders) ordered his regular forces to ignore the 38th Parallel in a furious onslaught which took them as far as the Yalu River. During the first week in November, true to Chou En-lai's warning, Chinese "volunteers" counterattacked with such sudden fury as to hurl the United Nations forces back as much as 100 miles.

Despite this staggeringly successful coup, the Chinese forces suddenly and mysteriously withdrew, and for two weeks there was a lull on the northern front. This sudden abandonment of their campaign, when they were sweeping everything before them, gave both the Security Council and the General Assembly a chance to evaluate that new and startling development. They readily conceded that Chou En-lai had more than justified his warning. He had proved that the presence of United Nations forces close to the Chinese-Korean border was regarded by Peking as a direct menace to Chinese security.

The United States Asserts Its Influence

In order to allay this fear, President [Harry] Truman, on November 17, tried to assure the Chinese Government that neither the United States nor the United Nations had any aggressive designs against China. Two days later the Peking Government made it plain in a radio broadcast from Peking that no credence was placed in Mr. Truman's protestations. The broadcaster insisted that America had lied and smashed its way across the world into Chinese territory, had seized Formosa [now known as Taiwan], and was threatening another neighbor, Indo-China [now known as Vietnam]. In a subsequent note to the United Nations, the Peking Government justified its aid to North Korea as a means of repelling American aggression. On November 22, in a further effort to allay Chinese fear and suspicions, Great Britain, through her Charge d'Affaires [diplomat] in Peking, reaffirmed United Nations objectives in Korea and insisted that they posed no threat to Chinese security or interest in that area.

(Incidentally, the earnest protestations to the Chinese that neither Manchuria nor any other Chinese territory would be encroached upon either by the United States or by England were enough in themselves to excite Chinese suspicions. For example, one of President Truman's first and most hope-inspiring announcements after World War II was that America would not claim any indemnity or one foot of territory incident to her part in that war. Whatever his promptings may have been, that announcement was quickly followed by a decree that we would establish military bases throughout the Pacific. First, they were to be safeguards against any possible military resurgence of the Japanese. Then they were to be against any possible encroachments by Russia. But they were all glaring *American* encroachments upon Asiatic soil.)

U.S. Forces Are Repelled

On September 24, after allegedly announcing that he would have the boys home by Christmas, and apparently regarding Chinese inactivity as evidence that their forces were disintegrating, General MacArthur launched a major offensive for a quick ending of the conflict, the action extending into territory close to and along the full length of the Chinese frontier. The inert Chinese responded with a sudden and ferocious counter-offensive which threatened to engulf the Allied forces, and sent them reeling back to positions far to the South. Although the Chinese had done absolutely nothing except adhere to the warning plainly given by Chou En-lai on October 5, on November 28 General MacArthur complained to the Security Council that "an entirely new war is now facing the United Nations forces." On that same day, General Wu Hsiu-chuan,

Peking's representative, appeared before the Security Council. He refused to answer charges of Chinese aggression directed at him by the United States representative, Warren R. Austin, repeated China's accusation of American aggression, and justified the actions of the Chinese "volunteers" who had crossed into Korea for helping to liberate the Korean people.

On December 14, the Security Council adopted a resolution offered by an Asian-Arab group to "determine the basis on which a satisfactory cease-fire in Korea can be arranged." President of the Assembly, Nasrollah Entesam of Iran, named Sir Benegal Rau [of India] and Lester B. Pearson, Canada's Secretary of State for External Affairs, to serve with him as a three-man committee for working out and implementing the terms of that resolution. Since the smiles of Mars [Roman god of war] were still most decidedly for the Chinese, and perhaps more or less influenced by Russia, the first reply of the Peking Government expressed a fear that this new approach represented nothing but a scheme for enabling the Allies to regroup and consolidate. Upon a request by the Prime Ministers of the Canadian and British Governments for additional clarification of their reply, however, the Chinese issued a second statement accepting in principle the idea that a cease-fire arrangement should be the first order of business before a seven-nation conference, as suggested by the Good Offices Committee.

China Is Acting in Its Own Best Interest

The United States flatly rejected that proposition as "a transparent effort to divide the free world," and countered with a demand that China be branded as an aggressor against Korea. Other United Nations members refused to agree to this demand unless and until it was so worded as to be purely moral and to embrace no punitive measures. Even when it came to a vote, Mr. Pearson termed it "premature and unwise." Sir Benegal Rau predicted that it would end all chances for a negotiated peace. [Political commentator] Walter Lippmann, noting that the vote revealed that America had no important supporters in Asia, said, "The victory for which Mr. Austin said he thanked God is a self-inflicted American defeat." It will be recalled that China's immediate reaction was a flat assertion that unless that stigma was retracted, she would engage in no more peace talks while any foreign forces remained on Korean soil. Once more, the Chinese were merely doing what they had given due notice that they would do.

It is thus seen from this highly attenuated review of the issues between America and China subsequent to December that they add up to nothing but a bitter charge of aggression of each against the other. It must be clear to any unbiased person that this is far from a one-sided question. Suppose we look facts squarely in the face—for once. The Monroe Doctrine, 1823, declares, in substance, that the attempt of any European power to gain a foothold in the western hemisphere (no Asiatic power could so much as register a thought in that connection) will be regarded as "an unfriendly disposition towards the United States."

In the name of reason, why should not the Asiatics feel even more concern when a Power from the antipodes [a person or power from the opposite side of the globe] attempts to impose its demands upon their own ethnic brothers, and upon their own native soil? Any arguments to the contrary seem to me to be running counter to every attribute of human nature and common sense. Assuming that the Chinese are normal human beings (and I see nothing naive in such an assumption), it seems unthinkable that they would elect indefinitely to devastate their own country, and die like flies (Brig. Gen. John H. Michaelis reported on May 14 that Red China units, some of them fifteen-year-old boys, others old men, hunchbacks, and cripples had gone into battle, only about half of whom had rifles, the others being equipped with hand grenades), for the sheer diversion of waging an *aggressive war* on their own soil against an inoffensive and peace-seeking America.

While Communist Russia is understandably in full sympathy with Communist China, and (thanks to America's precedent of lavishing military aid upon the enemies of nominally friendly nations) now seems to be increasing its aid to the Chinese, the very suggestion that these Chinese are so idiotic as to continue wading through the hell which now engulfs them, at the mere behest of Russia—a line of propaganda now being pursued in America *ad nauseam* [to an excessive degree]—seems preposterous on its very face. Even MacArthur declared emphatically before the Senate Investigating Committee on May 6 that ". . . the linking of the Soviet to this Korean war paled out as the events have progressed." It seems equally absurd—though less selfless—for America to persist in expending thousands of lives, billions of dollars, pauperizing its own citizens and flirting with a Third World War, for the fantastic purpose of imposing its will upon antipodeans. This is doubly disturbing, since it is making hopeless enemies of the once friendly Asiatics and alienating large segments of Europe's population.

A Clash over Name-Calling

Lest we forget, let it once more be stressed that this entire battle to the last ditch, the last dollar and the last human expendable boils down to nothing more nor less than a clash over name-calling. When, in December, the carnage was becoming frightfully contrary to America's calculations, and after the terms upon which China finally agreed to discuss peace were denounced by us as *appeasements* (a much abused term), we irascibly countered by forcing upon China the brand of *aggressor.* China promptly and irascibly returned the compliment, and expressed a determination, in effect, to engage in no more peace talks while that stigma remained. Thus (despite America's persistent plaint that China is merely acting as Russia's puppet) it becomes undebatable that this entire nightmarish situation could have been eradicated virtually overnight through the mere abjuration of that offensive and double-edged charge of aggression.

Since it was America's direct and precipitate action which brought about this stalemate and slaughter, it seems clear that it was much more her duty before the world than that of China to do the abjuring which would have promptly ended it. Let it once more be stressed that our most important European allies bitterly opposed that provocative, if not baseless affront to China. Sir Benegal Rau sagely and prophetically warned that it ended all hope for a negotiated peace. Walter Lippmann termed it "America's self-imposed defeat." Therefore, since that hasty and ill-advised slap at China brought nothing but a hopeless stalemate in slaughter, destruction, impoverishment, and steadily mounting war hysteria, it would seem to be up to this nation to make the first move toward cutting the Gordian knot [an insolvable problem]. If both sides, or either side, would rather persist in the preposterous farce of "saving face," in the puerile pretense of not knowing exactly why the other is fighting, or to what end, than to thus simply save their nationals from further slaughter and pauperization, then I can only paraphrase a derogatory ditty of yesteryear:

"If that's what you call sanity, excuse me!"

Unspeakable Tragedy

Incidentally, it was revealed through the MacArthur-Congressional controversy that the United Nations circles became greatly perturbed over the possibility that crossing the 38th Parallel might force China and perhaps Russia into that Korean conflict. When, on May 3, Senator Brion McMahon asked MacArthur if he had thought there would be any such development, he replied: "I doubted it." He also countered with this question of his own: "Would the Soviet desire to have China become so powerful that it might challenge the Soviet?" On that same day a press report read: ". . . the President was reminded that there seemed to be an air of optimism at Wake Island last October after the discussion with MacArthur that the Korean war would be cleaned up soon. He was asked if this feeling was based upon the belief that the Chinese would not enter the Korean war. It was then that the President said MacArthur certainly persuaded him that the Chinese would not move."

In his testimony before the Senate Investigating Committee on May 25, General J. Lawton Collins, Army Chief of Staff, according to the United Press, made the unqualified statement that ". . . on September 27 a 'directive' was sent to MacArthur ordering him not to cross the border and, 'as a matter of policy,' to use nothing but South Korean troops 'in the northeast provinces bordering on the Soviet Union or in the area along the Manchurian border. . . .'"

It is disturbing that General Collins refrained from revealing to his inquisitors and to the American people the exact developments back of these directives to MacArthur. It is doubly disturbing that the most bitter and captious partisans to both sides of this controversy seemed to be in complete accord regarding one policy. It was on the policy of remaining as mute as mummies about Chou En-lai's dire warning of October 5 that: "The Chinese people will not stand idly by and see their neighbors ruthlessly invaded" across the 38th Parallel. Why, fellow-victims and doom dodgers? Why! Why!! Why!!! Such seeming obtuseness to or contempt for the glaring, direct, and self-evident cause of that Korean stalemate, with its sickening toll of blood and treasure, should at least give pause to all who fain would know exactly why Americans are thus being slaughtered by the thousands, pauperized by the millions, and having their futures warped and mortgaged for ages to come over perfectly nebulous issues in the antipodes. The unspeakable tragedy of this whole miserable mess is that the havoc which has already been wrought, and the unmitigated hell which awaits the future, stem from the preposterous and discredited hysteria that Russia is master-minding and gloating over it as the prelude to her own worldwide war of aggression.

Korea Needs U.S. Aid to Fend Off Communist Aggression

Y.T. Pyun

Foreign Minister Y.T. Pyun, who was appointed as South Korea's acting prime minister in 1953, believed that Korea was at the center of a conflict larger than the Korean War. Pyun agreed with U.S. officials that the Soviets looked to the resources of Asia as a springboard to the eventual conquest of Western Europe. Pyun believed that if the United States supported Korea, world security could be maintained. The following speech was presented before the nonprofit relief organization Cooperative for American Relief Everywhere (CARE). CARE provides food, water, health care, and other emergency assistance to countries in need.

You all know that Korea has been unfortunately caught in the global conflict between the world-conquest-dreaming communism and the survival-seeking democracy. She has been caught in the vortex of world disturbance, of violence and destruction, quite helpless and unprepared—unprepared except in her indomitable spirit and unswerving determination to die fighting on the side of human freedom. Sometimes I quite dispassionately ask: Had there existed no Korea, would this conflict have been averted? It would have broken out somewhere else, say, in Iran or in Vietnam or in Burma, or even in India. No matter where the aggression appeared, its nature would have been the same—of communist global conquest. Any meaningful action on the part of the free world counteracting aggression of this nature must, therefore, be designed on a global level. No matter where it appears, the aggression must be met firmly and thoroughly with the total weight of the free world. Nothing should stand in our way to a swift and complete military victory. All military half-measures should be carefully eschewed, for they are bound to invite further aggression.

We Are Fighting the Free World's Battles

We Koreans do not pretend to understand the position so far taken either by England or by India. They look to us like a patient insisting on a "head-first" treatment when his hand has been invaded by germs of a deadly disease. We are now fighting England's as well as India's battle in Korea. If we are defeated, the struggle will be carried to their own homes. If we come out victorious, they will have no war at home.

The Soviet Union has deliberately chosen Asia as its first object of conquest. Its very first stroke has been deliberately planted on Korea, a long-coveted strategic point, from which naval operations can be launched to tear up the Pacific traffic of the free world and which will prove an ideal watchtower to keep the whole Orient, including China and Japan, under the domineering glance of the Soviet Union.

To the cool, calculating mind of the Kremlin [Soviets] the conquest of western Europe is unthinkable until the vast resources of Asia are consolidated under its domination. The conquest of Asia alone will condition the Kremlin to launch an all-out global conquest. The formula of remedy should appear to be: Balk the Kremlin in the attainment of this pre-requisite, and the dreaded thing will never come off. There is every reason that England, doing away with her local-mindedness, should send more troops to Korea now and that India, too, should start sending them. The weak-jointed dinosaur will recede before nothing but a drawn sword. In the vacuum of indecision alone, the Soviet balloon of threat will wax larger.

The level-headed [Soviet premier Joseph] Stalin knows that he lacks fuel oil, that he lacks such mobility as is known in the United States, and that he lacks even the loyalty of his own people and of those of his satellites. Above all, he is well aware that this time he will have to go without the American Lend-Lease [a program during World War II in which the United States assisted nations that were fighting the Axis powers], which played such a decisive role in his successful struggle against Germany. Nothing short of the fear of provoking the United-States-led free world into a general war will stop the Stalinist aggression in Asia. That Iran is now confronted with somewhat the same situation as has developed in Korea may be said to be the direct result of the restricted and therefore indecisive military action in Korea.

It Will Not Stop Here

Before I end this general survey of the world situation, of which the present Korean war is a local manifestation, I should like to draw your attention to the fact that the one changing motive behind all the Soviet tactics of playing hot and cold, fast and loose, with the free world, getting it on crisis after crisis and letting it off as often at will, is, through a series of serious economic dislocations, to create within free nations situations where the Soviet Union can more easily take over from within. My advice is, therefore, this: Don't be let down this time; see that the international criminal does not get away unpunished this once, whatever happens. Now I am coming to relief at last. Except the few towns of considerable size, located in the area which, from the beginning of the war, has never been harried by the enemy and which, in area, is not more than one-thirtieth of entire Korea, most of the towns in the bulk of South Korea and in North Korea have been taken and retaken by both contending forces and a large number of them have been completely laid waste beyond recognition. Because the United Nations forces have been forbidden to cross the Manchurian [Chinese] border and blow up enemy supply centers, all they have been doing is to pound away to smithereens all buildings and houses that are likely to give shelter to the enemy.

Except the few millions who either have remained protected behind the UN defence line or have been fortunate enough to filter through it from beyond, the bulk of the Korean people, rendered homeless and uprooted, as it were, out of the soil, wander like clouds over areas made desolate by the war and vanish like clouds, exposed to hunger, cold and man-made demolition. Just think of a full-fledged modern war of hither-to-unheard-of power of destruction again and again sweeping over such a narrow strip of land as Korea for the last ten months. Just think of scores of thousands of tons of high explosives smashing up nothing but Korea! Neither Germany nor Japan, war-harried as they were, can approach the present Korea in stark devastation. The Korean case, in which her allies, in terms of practicalities, seem to have joined hands with her enemies in her own destruction, partly out of regard for her deadly foes, is something tragically unique and unparalleled in human history.

This bleak past lies unrelieved by any immediate bright future. This spring sowing season finds the bulk of agricultural soil untilled and unsowed for lack of work beasts or of farm laborers or of huts that shelter them or even of seed.

The problems of relief thus posed by a nation-wide destruction and by an entire nation turned refugees are overwhelming. The United Nations Command has been doing all that was humanly possible, but the number of refugees it reached and saved is a mere fraction of the masses who roam homeless and perish as they roam and who perish unseen and unsuccored in remote outlying places. The United Nations Command ought not to be expected to attempt relief to the extent of military insecurity. It cannot make an outlay sufficient to meet the relief demands, either in personnel or in transportation or otherwise. The inexorable demands of military operations, to which the United Nations Command is dutybound to give priorities, are apt to keep its hands too full for anything like adequate relief for civilians. The need has long been felt for fuller and more active cooperation of all available civilian relief agencies of the free world with the United Nations Command and of creation of a far wider opening admitting these civilian agencies more freely into Korea. It is indeed gratifying that CARE [Cooperative for American Relief Everywhere] plans to make a nation-wide appeal for Korean relief and spearhead civilian relief activities for the suffering millions in Korea.

In view of the overtaxed military transportation, overtaxed even for military purposes alone, Korean relief, in order to be extensive and nation-widely penetrating, must be provided with a minimum transportation of its own, both land and sea. Under the circumstances, certain main arteries of land traffic and main harbor facilities are bound to remain exclusive to military purposes. But byways and small ports should be available for relief activities. The civilian relief personnel may need to be men of as much valor as combat teams, very probably of a higher order. They may be irked by the necessary screening exercised by the appropriate authorities. But I do not doubt that the American public, when once roused to a very pressing need, will not fail as it never did in the past to rise to meet it like one man, sweeping every obstacle or inconvenience before it.

The Korean people are now undergoing a virtual genocide, which should not be unnecessarily complete. The present humanitarian movement you are now setting your hands to, if given momentum promptly enough, will save millions of Koreans who otherwise are doomed to perish. As the Foreign Minister of the Republic of Korea, I feel I must pay tribute also at this time to the American Red Cross, which so instantly responded to my President's plea for help soon after the invasion of June, 1950. I am gratified to learn that the American Relief for Korea Committee is actually engaged in this humanitarian effort to relieve the suffering of the Korean people. I will always remember you in my prayers that God may speed your worthy efforts to instantaneous fruition.

The Situation Grows Grave

I started out to give you a general view of the Korean situation, and it may not be out of place here to suggest to you the outstanding needs other than that of relief. I will briefly enumerate four more needs without troubling you as to their order of importance.

Korea is badly in need of financial aid, distinct from economic aid, that will go to stabilize her now fast-crumbling finance. It is true that she has a balanced budget, but balanced on paper only. All sound budgets are based on assured national revenues. Almost all the Korean sources of revenue lie shattered and disrupted by the war. A complete measure of rehabilitation alone will restore them, but that is not forthcoming under the circumstances. What was opportunely done for Greece to bolster its finance must be done now for Korea. [Under the Truman Doctrine, the United States lent assistance to Greece to keep the nation from falling to Communist insurgency.]

Another need for Korea is more arms for the pending military expansion program. We do not object to rearming Japan, so long as Japanese are not brought over to Korea to fight in our place. To say the least, it will help Korean Communists strut as patriots fighting the age-long Korean enemy, and, at the same time, dishearten the ROK [Republic of Korea] forces so as to lower their fighting morale. Nor do we relish the idea of having the Chinese Nationalist troops among the UN forces now fighting in Korea, for we know that they can be more profitably used elsewhere, when the occasion arises. What we lack is arms, not manpower. It will be a grievance to Korea, if she is denied the chance of contributing more manpower to the cause of human freedom— the only contribution she can make as far as circumstances allow her now.

The third need is for technically training as many intelligent young Koreans as possible. In view of the fact that what scanty trained Korean personnel we had before have been mostly captured, killed or incapacitated during the present war, any long-range plan for Korea cannot overlook the crying need for an extensive training program, without which any rehabilitation of an enduring nature is impossible. It is wrong to keep them all in Korea. There are not arms enough to go round. Nor are there any munition factories to absorb their energies and make them contribute to war efforts. I personally do not see the sense of letting them rot by slamming upon them the door that leads them abroad for qualifying them for services of no less value to the nation than fighting. Anyway, they cannot all fight.

Compared with the thousands of Japanese receiving technical training in this country, there is an ever-dwindling number of Korean youths given the same academic benefits, mere dozens for the year. Considering the disparity of technical attainment existing between the two peoples under discussion, the reverse of the ratio would seem fair. The training of Korean industrial personnel should be given more candid consideration. I regard it to be one of the obligations of the free world to train and conserve an adequate number of Korean young men in the industrial way.

The MacArthur Line

Lastly I call your attention to the peremptory need of perpetuating in the proposed Japanese peace treaty in clear terms the present high seas demarkation between Korea and Japan, known as the MacArthur line. The line was instituted for sound reasons which will grow sounder as Japan gets out of the occupation status. From immemorial times up to the opening-up of Korea for world trade, it was the Japanese fishing boats that incessantly harried and plundered hamlets and towns on the Korean coast, which eventually paved the way for the Hideyoshi Invasion, the greatest national calamity known in our history. In [the] future, Japanese fishing boats will probably find it advisable to refrain from downright vandalism, but, if allowed to come close enough to Korean territorial waters, they might easily turn into moving bases for smuggling, so as to nip the viability of [the] Korean economy in the bud.

I do personally know of cases where large Japanese fishing boats, infringing the MacArthur line, attempted to butt Korean naval patrols into the sea. It is the established practice with the small Korean fishing vessels to scurry away into safety whenever powerful Japanese ships are sighted on their side of the demarcation, for they know there is always the treacherous sea to bear the Japanese blame of foundering them unseen by Law. The abolishment of the line would mean not only stymieing the nascent Korean fishing enterprise but also placing the entire Korean economy at the mercy of Japanese commercial aggression. While Korea is quite prepared to see Japan restored to its rightful place among the family of nations, she cannot afford to consent to any agreement or non-agreement, for that matter, that leaves open an avenue through which Japan can dictate the very subsistence of Korea. Korea cannot be persuaded to forego the only and real safeguard she has against possible Japanese economic aggression.

In Bataan, people from two different races fought their common foe, interlocked in comradeship and common ideals. In the world Bataan called Korea the brave sons of numerous free nations blend their honoured ashes in an everlasting covenant of cooperation for one single end— the preservation of free ways of life—which, we fervently hope, will be strengthened with time. Remember that, in this case, there is no world Australia from which to base a military comeback. The free world cannot afford to retreat from this world Bataan.

Korea is a unique exception. Of all small peoples, she is the only one that boldly threw its lot with the free nations, under most unimaginable circumstances of adversity. Proportionately, in terms of sacrifice, she has contributed most of all to the cause of human freedom. It may be no more than the widow's mite. But it is also true that she has dedicated all to the cause, which she can call her own.

Whether Korea was wise in putting up a heroic fight

against Communism, alias decivilization, or the now Soviet satellites were comparatively wiser in succumbing to Communism unresisting will be eventually decided by the part played by the free world in the wartime relief as well as in the post-war rehabilitation of Korea. If the direction now being pointed to by CARE is persistently and intensively pursued, Korea, I am certain, will stand, not a battered tomb of freedom but a proud monument eternally bearing witness to the triumph of free human will.

2

THE KOREAN WAR
AND THE WORLD

The United States Must Engage in an All-Out War with Korea

Douglas MacArthur

On April 11, 1951, President Harry Truman relieved General Douglas MacArthur of his post as supreme commander of U.S. and UN troops in Korea. MacArthur had challenged Truman's authority by openly criticizing his limited war policy. MacArthur also undermined peace negotiations between Korean and U.S./UN officials by issuing an unauthorized statement threatening the Communists if they refused to accept the terms being offered to them. Despite MacArthur's dismissal, he was given a hero's welcome in the United States and was asked to address a joint session of Congress. MacArthur gave a thirty-seven-minute speech, closing it with a line from an old army ballad: "Old soldiers never die—they just fade away." The chambers, which had been fully packed, gave MacArthur standing ovations before, during, and after his speech.

Mr. President, Mr. Speaker, and Distinguished Members of the Congress

I stand on this rostrum with a sense of deep humility and great pride—humility in the wake of those great American architects of our history who have stood here before me, pride in the reflection that this forum of legislative debate represents human liberty in the purest form yet devised. Here are centered the hopes and aspirations and faith of the entire human race.

Douglas MacArthur, address to a joint session of Congress, Washington, DC, April 19, 1951.

I do not stand here as advocate for any partisan cause for the issues are fundamental and reach quite beyond the realm of partisan consideration. They must be resolved on the highest plane of national interest if our course is to prove sound and our future protected. I trust, therefore, that you will do me the justice of receiving that which I have to say as solely expressing the considered viewpoint of a fellow American. I address you with neither rancor nor bitterness in the fading twilight of life with but one purpose in mind—to serve my country.

The Communist Threat Is a Global One
The issues are global and so interlocked that to consider the problems of one sector, oblivious to those of another, is but to court disaster for the whole. While Asia is commonly referred to as the gateway to Europe, it is no less true that Europe is the gateway to Asia. And the broad influence of the one cannot fail to have its impact upon the other.

There are those who claim our strength is inadequate to protect on both fronts—that we cannot divide our effort. I can think of no greater expression of defeatism. If a potential enemy can divide his strength on two fronts it is for us to counter his effort. The Communist threat is a global one. Its successful advance in one sector threatens the destruction of every other sector. You cannot appease or otherwise surrender to Communism in Asia without simultaneously undermining our efforts to halt its advance in Europe. . . .

Of more direct and immediate bearing upon our national security are the changes wrought in the strategic potential of the Pacific Ocean in the course of the past war. Prior thereto, the Western strategic frontier of the United States lay on the littoral line of the Americas with an exposed island salient extending out through Hawaii, Midway and Guam to the Philippines. That salient proved not an outpost of strength but an avenue of weakness along which the enemy could and did attack. The Pacific was a potential area of advance for any predatory force intent upon striking at the bordering land areas.

All this was changed by our Pacific victory. Our strategic frontier then shifted to embrace the entire Pacific Ocean which became a vast moat to protect us as long as we hold it. Indeed, it acts as a protective shield for all of the Americas and all free lands of the Pacific Ocean area. We control it to the shores of Asia by a chain of islands extending in an arc from the Aleutians to the Mariannas held by us and our free allies. From this island chain we can dominate with sea and air power every Asiatic port from Vladivostock to Singapore and prevent any hostile movement into the Pacific. Any predatory attack from Asia must be an amphibious effort. No amphibious force can be successful without control of the sea lanes and the air over those lanes in its avenue of advance. With naval and air supremacy and modest ground elements to defend bases, any major attack from continental Asia toward us or our friends of the Pacific would be doomed to failure. Under such conditions the Pacific no longer represents menacing avenues of approach for a prospective invader—it assumes instead the friendly aspect of a peaceful lake. Our line of defense is a natural one and can be maintained with a minimum of military effort and expense. It envisions no attack against anyone nor does it provide the bastions essential for offensive operations, but properly maintained would be an invincible defense against aggression.

We Must Protect One to Protect All

The holding of this littoral defense line in the Western Pacific is entirely dependent upon holding all segments thereof, for any major breach of that line by an unfriendly power would render vulnerable to determined attack every other major segment. This is a military estimate as to which I have yet to find a military leader who will take exception. For that reason I have strongly recommended in the past as a matter of military urgency that under no circumstances must Formosa [now known as Taiwan] fall under Communist control. Such an eventuality would at once threaten the freedom of the Philippines and the loss of Japan, and might well force our Western frontier back to the coasts of California, Oregon and Washington.

To understand the changes which now appear upon the Chinese mainland, one must understand the changes in Chinese character and culture over the past fifty years. China up to fifty years ago was completely non-homogeneous, being compartmented into groups divided against each other. The war-making tendency was almost non-existent, as they still followed the tenets of the Confucian ideal of pacifist culture. At the turn of the century, under the regime of Chan So Lin, efforts toward greater homogeneity produced the start of a nationalist urge. This was further and more successfully developed under the leadership of Chiang Kai Shek [head of the Chinese Nationalist government], but has been brought to its greatest fruition under the present regime, to the point that it has now taken on the character of a united nationalism of increasingly dominant aggressive tendencies. Through these past fifty years, the Chinese people have thus become militarized in their concepts and in their ideals. They now constitute excellent soldiers with competent staffs and commanders. This has produced a new and dominant power in Asia which for its own purposes is allied with Soviet Russia, but which in its own concepts and methods has become agressively imperialistic with a lust for expansion and increased power normal to this type of imperialism. There is little of the ideological concept either one way or another in the Chinese makeup. The standard of living is so low and the capital accumulation has been so thoroughly dissipated by war that the masses are desperate and avid to follow any leadership which seems to promise the alleviation of local stringencies. I have from the beginning believed that the Chinese Communists' support of the North Koreans was the dominant one. Their interests are at present parallel to those of the Soviet, but I believe that the aggressiveness recently displayed not only in Korea, but also in Indo-China [now known as Vietnam] and Tibet and pointing potentially toward the South, reflects predominantly the same lust for the expansion of power which has animated every would-be conqueror since the beginning of time. . . .

On Formosa, the government of the Republic of China has had the opportunity to refute by action much of the malicious gossip which so undermined the strength of its leadership on the Chinese mainland. The Formosan people are receiving a just and enlightened administration with majority representation on the organs of government, and politically, economically and socially they appear to be advancing along sound and constructive lines. . . .

The Korean Conflict

I now turn to the Korean conflict. While I was not consulted prior to the President's decision to intervene in support of the Republic of Korea [South Korea], that decision, from a military standpoint, proved a sound one as we hurled back the invader and decimated his forces. Our victory was complete and our objectives within reach when Red China intervened with numerically superior ground forces. This created a new war and an entirely new situation—a situation not contemplated when our forces were committed against the North Korean invaders—a situation which called for new decisions in the diplomatic sphere to permit the realistic adjustment of military strategy. Such decisions have not been forthcoming. While no man in his right mind would advocate sending our ground forces into continental China and such was never given a thought, the new situation did urgently demand a drastic revision of strategic planning if our political aim was to defeat this new enemy as we had defeated the old.

Apart from the military need as I saw it, to neutralize the sanctuary protection given the enemy north of the Yalu [River, which runs between North Korea and China], I felt that military necessity in the conduct of the war made mandatory:

1. The intensification of our economic blockade against China;
2. The imposition of a naval blockade against the China coast;

3. Removal of restrictions on air reconnaissance of China's coastal areas and of Manchuria;
4. Removal of restrictions on the forces of the Republic of China on Formosa with logistical support to contribute to their effective operations against the common enemy.

For entertaining these views, all professionally designed to support our forces committed to Korea and bring hostilities to an end with the least possible delay and at a saving of countless American and Allied lives, I have been severely criticized in lay circles, principally abroad, despite my understanding that from a military standpoint the above views have been fully shared in the past by practically every military leader concerned with the Korean campaign, including our own Joint Chiefs of Staff.

Not Enough Support to Finish the Job

I called for reinforcements, but was informed that reinforcements were not available. I made clear that if not permitted to destroy the enemy build-up bases north of the Yalu; if not permitted to utilize the friendly Chinese force of some six hundred thousand men on Formosa; if not permitted to blockade the China coast to prevent the Chinese Reds from getting succor [reinforcement of troops] from without; and if there were to be no hope of major reinforcements, the position of the command from the military standpoint forbade victory. We could hold in Korea by constant maneuver and at an approximate area where our supply line advantages were in balance with the supply line disadvantages of the enemy, but we could hope at best for only an indecisive campaign, with its terrible and constant attrition upon our forces if the enemy utilized his full military potential. I have constantly called for the new political decisions essential to a solution. Efforts have been made to distort my position. It has been said that I was in effect a warmonger. Nothing could be further from the truth. I know war as few other men now living know it, and nothing to me is more revolting. I have long advocated its complete abolition as its very destructiveness on both friend and foe has rendered it useless as a means of settling international disputes. . . . But once war is forced upon us, there is no other alternative than to apply every available means to bring it to a swift end. War's very object is victory—not prolonged indecision. In war, indeed, there can be no substitute for victory.

Appeasement Will Not Solve Our Problem

There are some who for varying reasons would appease Red China. They are blind to history's clear lesson. For history teaches with unmistakable emphasis that appeasement but begets new and bloodier war. It points to no single instance where the end has justified that means—where appeasement has led to more than a sham peace. Like blackmail, it lays the basis for new and successively greater demands, until, as in blackmail, violence becomes the only other alternative. Why, my soldiers asked of me, surrender military advantages to an enemy in the field? I could not answer. Some may say to avoid spread of the conflict into an all-out war with China; others, to avoid Soviet intervention. Neither explanation seems valid. For China is already engaging with the maximum power it can commit and the Soviet will not necessarily mesh its actions with our moves. Like a cobra, any new enemy will more likely strike whenever it feels that the relativity in military or other potential is in its favor on a world-wide basis.

The tragedy of Korea is further heightened by the fact that as military action is confined to its territorial limits, it condemns that nation, which it is our purpose to save, to suffer the devastating impact of full naval and air bombardment, while the enemy's sanctuaries are fully protected from such attack and devastation. Of the nations of the world, Korea alone, up to now, is the sole one which has risked its all against Communism. The magnificence of the courage and fortitude of the Korean people defies description. They have chosen to risk death rather than slavery. Their last words to me were "Don't scuttle the Pacific."

I have just left your fighting sons in Korea. They have met all tests there and I can report to you without reservation they are splendid in every way. It was my constant effort to preserve them and end this savage conflict honorably and with the least loss of time and a minimum sacrifice of life. Its growing bloodshed has caused me the deepest anguish and anxiety. Those gallant men will remain often in my thoughts and in my prayers always.

I am closing my fifty-two years of military service. When I joined the Army even before the turn of the century, it was the fulfillment of all my boyish hopes and dreams. The world has turned over many times since I took the oath on the plain at West Point and the hopes and dreams have long since vanished. But I still remember the refrain of one of the most popular barrack ballads of that day which proclaimed most proudly that:

"Old soldiers never die—they just fade away." And like the old soldier of that ballad, I now close my military career and just fade away—an old soldier who tried to do his duty as God gave him the light to see that duty.

Limiting the War in Korea Is Essential to Avoid a World War

Harry S. Truman

President Harry S. Truman made the following address as a partial response to General Douglas MacArthur's speech before Congress, excerpted in the previous selection. Truman clarifies U.S. objectives in Korea and the severe consequences of expanding the war.

I want to talk plainly to you tonight about what we are doing in Korea and about our policy in the Far East.

In the simplest terms, what we are doing in Korea is this: We are trying to prevent a third world war.

I think most people in this country recognized that fact [in] June [1950]. And they warmly supported the decision of the Government to help the Republic of Korea against the Communist aggressors. Now, many persons, even some who applauded our decision to defend Korea, have forgotten the basic reason for our action.

It is right for us to be in Korea. It was right last June. It is right today.

I want to remind you why this is true.

The Communist Threat to Freedom

The Communists in the Kremlin are engaged in a monstrous conspiracy to stamp out freedom all over the world. If they were to succeed, the United States would be numbered among their principal victims. It must be clear to

Harry S. Truman, televised address to the people of the United States, Washington, DC, April 16, 1951.

everyone that the United States cannot—and will not—sit idly by and await foreign conquest. The only question is: When is the best time to meet the threat and how?

The best time to meet the threat is in the beginning. It is easier to put out a fire in the beginning when it is small than after it has become a roaring blaze.

And the best way to meet the threat of aggression is for the peace-loving nations to act together. If they don't act together, they are likely to be picked off, one by one.

If they had followed the right policies in the 1930's—if the free countries had acted together, to crush the aggression of the dictators, and if they had acted in the beginning, when the aggression was small—there probably would have been no World War II.

If history has taught us anything, it is that aggression anywhere in the world is a threat to peace everywhere in the world. When that aggression is supported by the cruel and selfish rulers of a powerful nation who are bent on conquest, it becomes a clear and present danger to the security and independence of every free nation.

This is a lesson that most people in this country have learned thoroughly. This is the basic reason why we joined in creating the United Nations. And since the end of World War II we have been putting that lesson into practice—we have been working with other free nations to check the aggressive designs of the Soviet Union before they can result in a third world war.

That is what we did in Greece, when that nation was threatened by the aggression of international communism.

The attack against Greece could have led to general war. But this country came to the aid of Greece. The United Nations supported Greek resistance. With our help, the determination and efforts of the Greek people defeated the attack on the spot.

Another big Communist threat to peace was the Berlin blockade. That too could have led to war. But again it was settled because free men would not back down in an emergency.

The Communist Plan for Conquest

The aggression against Korea is the boldest and most dangerous move the Communists have yet made.

The attack on Korea was part of a greater plan for conquering all of Asia.

I would like to read to you from a secret intelligence report which came to us after the attack. It is a report of a speech a Communist army officer in North Korea gave to a group of spies and saboteurs last May, one month before South Korea was invaded. The report shows in great detail how this invasion was part of a carefully prepared plot. Here is part of what the Communist officer, who had been trained in Moscow, told his men: "Our forces," he said, "are scheduled to attack South Korean forces about the middle of June. . . . The coming attack on South Korea marks the first step toward the liberation of Asia."

Notice that he used the word "liberation." That is Communist double-talk meaning "conquest."

I have another secret intelligence report here. This one tells what another Communist officer in the Far East told his men several months before the invasion of Korea. Here is what he said: "In order to successfully undertake the long awaited world revolution, we must first unify Asia. . . . Java, Indochina, Malaya, India, Tibet, Thailand, Philippines, and Japan are our ultimate targets. . . . The United States is the only obstacle on our road for the liberation of all countries in southeast Asia. In other words, we must unify the people of Asia and crush the United States."

That is what the Communist leaders are telling their people, and that is what they have been trying to do.

They want to control all Asia from the Kremlin.

This plan of conquest is in flat contradiction to what we believe. We believe that Korea belongs to the Koreans, that India belongs to the Indians—that all the nations of Asia should be free to work out their affairs in their own way. This is the basis of peace in the Far East and everywhere else.

The whole Communist imperialism is back of the attack on peace in the Far East. It was the Soviet Union that trained and equipped the North Koreans for aggression. The Chinese Communists massed 44 well-trained and well-equipped divisions on the Korean frontier. These were the troops they threw into battle when the North Korean Communists were beaten.

Stopping Short of General War

The question we have had to face is whether the Communist plan of conquest can be stopped without general war. Our Government and other countries associated with us in the United Nations believe that the best chance of stopping it without general war is to meet the attack in Korea and defeat it there.

That is what we have been doing. It is a difficult and bitter task.

But so far it has been successful.

So far, we have prevented World War III.

So far, by fighting a limited war in Korea, we have prevented aggression from succeeding and bringing on a general war. And the ability of the whole free world to resist Communist aggression has been greatly improved.

We have taught the enemy a lesson. He has found out that aggression is not cheap or easy. Moreover, men all over the world who want to remain free have been given new courage and new hope. They know now that the champions of freedom can stand up and fight and that they will stand up and fight.

Our resolute stand in Korea is helping the forces of freedom now fighting in Indochina [Vietnam] and other countries in that part of the world. It has already slowed down the timetable of conquest.

In Korea itself, there are signs that the enemy is building up his ground forces for a new mass offensive. We also know that there have been large increases in the enemy's available air forces.

If a new attack comes, I feel confident it will be turned back. The United Nations fighting forces are tough and able and well equipped. They are fighting for a just cause.

They are proving to all the world that the principle of collective security will work. We are proud of all these forces for the magnificent job they have done against heavy odds. We pray that their efforts may succeed, for upon their success may hinge the peace of the world.

The Communist side must now choose its course of action. The Communist rulers may press the attack against us. They may take further action which will spread the conflict. They have that choice, and with it the awful responsibility for what may follow. The Communists also have the choice of a peaceful settlement which could lead to a general relaxation of tensions in the Far East. The decision is theirs, because the forces of the United Nations will strive to limit the conflict if possible.

We do not want to see the conflict in Korea extended. We are trying to prevent a world war—not to start one. The best way to do that is to make it plain that we and the other free countries will continue to resist the attack.

The Best Course to Follow

But you may ask: Why can't we take other steps to punish the aggressor? Why don't we bomb Manchuria and China itself? Why don't we assist Chinese Nationalist troops [from Formosa, modern-day Taiwan] to land on the mainland of China?

If we were to do these things we would be running a very grave risk of starting a general war. If that were to happen, we would have brought about the exact situation we are trying to prevent.

If we were to do these things, we would become entangled in a vast conflict on the continent of Asia and our task would become immeasurably more difficult all over the world.

What would suit the ambitions of the Kremlin better than for our military forces to be committed to a full-scale war with Red China?

It may well be that, in spite of our best efforts, the Communists may spread the war. But it would be wrong—tragically wrong—for us to take the initiative in extending the war.

The dangers are great. Make no mistake about it. Behind the North Koreans and Chinese Communists in the front lines stand additional millions of Chinese soldiers. And behind the Chinese stand the tanks, the planes, the submarines, the soldiers, and the scheming rulers of the Soviet Union.

Our aim is to avoid the spread of the conflict.

The course we have been following is the one best calculated to avoid an all-out war. It is the course consistent with our obligation to do all we can to maintain international peace and security. Our experience in Greece and Berlin shows that it is the most effective course of action we can follow.

First of all, it is clear that our efforts in Korea can blunt the will of the Chinese Communists to continue the struggle. The United Nations forces have put up a tremendous fight in Korea and have inflicted very heavy casualties on the enemy. Our forces are stronger now than they have been before. These are plain facts which may discourage the Chinese Communists from continuing their attack.

Second, the free world as a whole is growing in military strength every day. In the United States, in Western Europe, and throughout the world, free men are alert to the Soviet threat and are building their defenses. This may discourage the Communist rulers from continuing the war in Korea— and from undertaking new acts of aggression elsewhere.

If the Communist authorities realize that they cannot defeat us in Korea, if they realize it would be foolhardy to widen the hostilities beyond Korea, then they may recognize the folly of continuing their aggression. A peaceful settlement may then be possible. The door is always open.

Then we may achieve a settlement in Korea which will not compromise the principles and purposes of the United Nations.

I have thought long and hard about this question of extending the war in Asia. I have discussed it many times with the ablest military advisers in the country. I believe with all my heart that the course we are following is the best course.

I believe that we must try to limit the war to Korea for these vital reasons: to make sure that the precious lives of our fighting men are not wasted; to see that the security of our country and the free world is not needlessly jeopardized; and to prevent a third world war.

Avoiding Confusion over U.S. Policy

A number of events have made it evident that General [Douglas] MacArthur did not agree with that policy. I have therefore considered it essential to relieve General MacArthur so that there would be no doubt or confusion as to the real purpose and aim of our policy.

It was with the deepest personal regret that I found myself compelled to take this action. General MacArthur is one of our greatest military commanders. But the cause of world peace is more important than any individual.

The change in commands in the Far East means no change whatever in the policy of the United States. We will carry on the fight in Korea with vigor and determination in an effort to bring the war to a speedy and successful conclusion.

The new commander, Lt. Gen. Matthew Ridgway, has already demonstrated that he has the great qualities of military leadership needed for this task.

We are ready, at any time, to negotiate for a restoration of peace in the area. But we will not engage in appeasement. We are only interested in real peace.

Real peace can be achieved through a settlement based on the following factors:

One: the fighting must stop.
Two: concrete steps must be taken to insure that the fighting will not break out again.
Three: there must be an end to the aggression.

A settlement founded upon these elements would open

the way for the unification of Korea and the withdrawal of all foreign forces.

In the meantime, I want to be clear about our military objective. We are fighting to resist an outrageous aggression in Korea. We are trying to keep the Korean conflict from spreading to other areas. But at the same time we must conduct our military activities so as to insure the security of our forces. This is essential if they are to continue the fight until the enemy abandons its ruthless attempt to destroy the Republic of Korea.

That is our military objective—to repel attack and to restore peace.

In the hard fighting in Korea, we are proving that collective action among nations is not only a high principle but a workable means of resisting aggression. Defeat of aggression in Korea may be the turning point in the world's search for a practical way of achieving peace and security.

The struggle of the United Nations in Korea is a struggle for peace.

The free nations have united their strength in an effort to prevent a third world war.

That war can come if the Communist rulers want it to come. But this Nation and its allies will not be responsible for its coming.

We do not want to widen the conflict. We will use every effort to prevent that disaster. And in so doing we know that we are following the great principles of peace, freedom, and justice.

The United States Must Use a Combination of Force, Negotiation, and Aid in Korea

Philip C. Jessup

The following is taken from an address by Philip C. Jessup, U.S. ambassador to the United Nations. At the time the speech was made, the United States had been involved in Korea for almost a year. The mounting losses had drawn criticism from the press about Truman's aggressive foreign policy. Jessup responds by criticizing the media's oversimplification of foreign policy in general, which he states is not only inaccurate but also helps support Soviet propaganda. Jessup reiterates that the objective of U.S. foreign policy is to seek peaceful resolutions first.

It would be fortunate if one could say that foreign policy is really very simple, but that would not be true. Foreign policy has to cover the whole world, which is full of complications. If we commonly used the expression "domestic policy" to describe everything our Government does in regard to agriculture, taxation, conservation, crime, interstate commerce, defense, veterans' affairs, finance, the mails, and the dozens of other governmental functions, we would find that domestic policy covered a less complicated bundle of problems than those which have to be met by our foreign policy. This is true because almost every subject which the Government deals with internally has its duplicate in

Philip C. Jessup, address to Union College, Schenectady, NY, February 23, 1951.

the international field. As the President said in his State of the Union message on January 8, 1951, "the state of our Nation is in great part the state of our friends and allies throughout the world." Foreign policy actually also must cover relations with our enemies as well.

Mr. [Elihu] Root, who had been Secretary of War, Secretary of State, and United States Senator from New York, and who therefore had a remarkably broad familiarity with public affairs, made some further wise comments which are pertinent today:

> There is one specially important result which should follow from such a popular understanding of foreign affairs. That is, a sense of public responsibility in speech and writing, or perhaps it would be better stated as a public sense of private responsibility for words used in discussing international affairs. . . . It cannot, however, be expected that every individual in a great democracy will naturally practice restraint. Political demagogues will seek popularity by public speeches, full of insult to foreign countries, and yellow [disreputable] journals will seek to increase their circulation by appeals to prejudice against foreigners. Hitherto these have been passed over because the speakers and writers were regarded as irresponsible, but if the democracy of which the speakers and publishers are a part is to control international intercourse that irresponsibility ends, and it is the business of the democracy to see to it that practices by its members which lead directly towards war are discouraged and condemned.

The Whole Story Is Not Being Told

In the course of the current debates on foreign policy, there has appeared a line of argument which is no less dangerous because its authors have been unwilling to be perfectly frank. One development of this theme has received wide circulation through its publication in a weekly magazine. The comment to which I refer is based on the following passage from the President's message on the State of the Union:

"If we build our strength—and we are building it—the Soviet rulers may face the facts and lay aside their plans to take over the world. That is what we hope will happen, and that is what we are trying to bring about. That is the only realistic road to peace."

This statement by the President was part of a general exposition of the aggressive policies of the Soviet Union and of the contrasting peaceful policies of the United States. He outlined three points in our foreign policy.

The first covered the economic assistance program which we are carrying out in various countries. The President showed that this was one of the most effective ways to counter the typical Soviet Communist propaganda and their subversive techniques. He reminded us of the tremendous effect of the Marshall Plan on the stabilization of the European countries. He pointed out the way in which our programs of economic development will help to meet the basic causes of human distress upon which Communist propaganda attempts to feed.

Secondly, he mentioned our military assistance to countries which want to defend themselves. Here he referred to the North Atlantic Treaty Organization. He referred to the courage and confidence inspired by the appointment of General [Dwight D.] Eisenhower. He pointed to the record of U.N. armed resistance to aggression in Korea and our general support for independent governments of Asia. In a later part of his speech he dwelt at length upon the essential need of our own great rearmament effort.

Thirdly, the President pointed out that our foreign policy program includes our determination to continue to work for peaceful settlements of international disputes. He repeated our willingness to engage in negotiations with the Soviet Union as well as with any one else. He repeated our fixed determination to avoid appeasement.

The attack upon this program is based upon a very different idea. This other idea is that the United States can save itself only by resorting to preventive war. This is the inescapable logic of the position even though the conclusion is hedged by saying that maybe war is inevitable and maybe it is not. This line of thinking is obviously based on the cowardly and defeatist attitude which thinks that the United States and the other countries of the free world have no strength whatever except the atomic bomb. It assumes that we are incapable of determination, that we cannot stand a prolonged effort, that there is no strength or value in the basic traditions and principles of our democracy and our way of life. To put it crudely, this line of argument is based on the theory that the American people have no guts. It argues that when we are faced by a brutal enemy we cannot hold out either in the struggle for men's minds or in the struggle to save their bodies from destruction.

The American people have not accepted these propositions. They have not given their government any mandate to go to war. On the contrary, the American people clearly believe in the policy of peace through strength which the President outlined.

Let us summarize again the essential points in that program and then look at the alternative.

The first point in the program is building defensive strength.

The second point is at least to keep open the possibility of negotiation. In the latest note sent by the United States, France, and the United Kingdom to the Soviet Union regarding a meeting of the Foreign Ministers we have again said that we are perfectly willing to sit down and talk with them and have urged them to agree really to explore the basic causes of tensions.

The third point is that these steps are designed to deter the Soviet Union from launching an attack on the rest of the world.

The fourth point is that if the Soviet Union insists upon forcing war upon the world, the steps we are taking will put us in the best possible position to defend ourselves and to gain the victory.

The fifth point is that if the Soviets are deterred from starting the war, we may find ourselves in a rather long period of armed truce. In such a period the program we are following will enable the United States at least to hold its own. Both reason and history tell us that the corrosive elements of self-destruction are potent in a totalitarian police state and not in our democracy.

The sixth point is that there may or may not be a change in Soviet policy, but if such a change does occur we will be in a position to take advantage of it.

The seventh point is that if there is no change in Soviet policy, we have not left undone anything which we ought to have done and we will have lost none of the essential strength of our position.

The only alternative course to follow would be to start a war against the Soviet Union now. That is the policy to which the irresponsibles would inevitably drive us even though they are afraid to admit the logical conclusion of their arguments and seek to conceal it.

The task of our foreign policy is to guide the United States along a road which will preserve peace so long as peace can be maintained with justice and freedom. The United States will fight, if necessary, to preserve freedom and justice, but it will not make war merely because the road to peace is inevitably long and hard and tiresome.

Many of those who attack the foreign policy of the United States seem to be quite indifferent to the fact that they are constantly supporting the propaganda of the Soviet Union. They seem bent on convincing the other peoples of the world—just as the Communist propaganda tries to convince them—that we are a country bankrupt in ideas, resources, and courage. The result of their propaganda, like the result of Communist propaganda, is to persuade some people that we are constantly losing and that Soviet imperialism is the "wave of the future." These people know in their hearts that this line is just as false when they utter it as when the Soviet Union utters it. For whatever motive or reason, however, they ignore the injury which they are doing to their country and to the whole cause of the free world. As Mr. Root said: "Such public expressions by our own citizens bring discredit upon our country and injure its business and imperil its peace. . . . They will practically cease whenever the American public really condemns and resents them so that neither public office nor newspaper advertising or circulation can be obtained by them."

Actually, if one reviews the results of American foreign policy one finds a situation very different from that which is pictured by the irresponsibles. As a result of the Marshall Plan, Europe has been rescued from its terrible postwar difficulties and the Communist attempt to capture Western European governments has been defeated all along the line. As a result of the North Atlantic Treaty, the countries of Western Europe, together with Canada and the United States, under the military leadership of General Eisenhower are creating a strong defensive force. As a result of the Truman Doctrine, Greece has been saved from the Communists and is now contributing strength to the general position of the free world. With assistance from our military aid program, Turkey is strong and resolute.

As a result of the President's courageous decision on June 25 and of the overwhelming support of the members of the United Nations, the flagrant aggression in Korea has been met by force and is in check. The Communist aggression in Korea has been branded as such by the General Assembly of the United Nations.

Not all of our problems have been solved. There always have been, and there always will be, unresolved problems in the international scene. Progress toward the solution of many of these problems is being made. In spite of the opposition of the Soviet Government, we are advancing in our effort to reestablish Germany and Japan as democratic members of the community of nations stripped of any possibility or desire for a return to the aggressive regimes which brought about their countries' downfall. In the Western Hemisphere a solid basis of collaboration with the American republics has grown steadily firmer. Next month the Foreign Ministers of all the American republics will meet in Washington to consolidate their efforts in meeting our common problems.

The Soviet Union Only Recognizes Force

There have been long periods in the history of American foreign policy when we were at peace and without anxiety that our disagreements with other governments might sharpen into war. For decades we devoted our energies to the perfection of plans and procedures for the pacific settlement of international disputes. Today we are confronted by the active hostility of a government which, despite its signature of the United Nations Charter, has consistently refused to resort to the traditional processes of pacific settlement—conciliation, mediation, arbitration, judicial settlement. The Soviet Union does not recognize any abstract concept of the rule of law or the impartial administration of justice. For them law and the administration of justice are merely the instruments of the all-powerful state. In actuality this means the Party and its controlling oligarchy. This attitude in international affairs reflects the barbaric crudity of its internal system which respects only force as personified in the police state. No philosophic verbiage can conceal this fact, which inevitably colors the whole face of international relations today. Fortunately, the United Nations remains as a focus for the efforts of the law-abiding community to maintain decent standards of international conduct. We have normal differences and disagreements from time to time with governments other than those of the Soviet bloc, but these issues do not poison our relationships. Nor does it deflect us from the great democratic principle of the equality of states. In spite of Communist provocations and domestic vilification it will remain the object and the obligation of American foreign policy to seek peaceful adjustments of all issues without surrender or appeasement. We must be strong and resourceful. Above all we must have the moral strength which comes from conviction in the rightness of our cause.

Saving Ourselves for the Big Battle Against Communism

John Dille

The Korean War ended with heavy loss of life and very little gain for either side after armistice. Few Americans at the time considered the cost worth the effort. But in his book *Substitute for Victory*, war correspondent John Dille writes that the Korean War was a success. Dille states that U.S. intervention was necessary to counter the threat posed by communism as well as gain insight into enemy tactics. Dille believes the Korean conflict was a way for the Soviet Union to wear down the United States, but fortunately the United States did not overcommit itself. By ending the war when it did, the United States saved its reserve for the inevitable final battle. Dille contends that communism could only be quashed by going right to the source: the Soviet Union and Red China.

Besides the military lesson which Korea taught us—that the biggest, most modern, and best equipped nation is not necessarily destined, *per se*, to win all its battles—we also learned a basic lesson in geopolitics which is a corollary to the military lesson: when two major forces are squared off against each other, as the free world and the Communist world were opposed in Korea, it requires more than token combat, no matter how determined, skillful, and morally sound it may be, to carry the day.

We have been lucky in our wars. We were successful against Germany on two different occasions. And we defeated the Japanese. As a result of these successes we came dangerously close to taking our luck for granted. We came to think of war as a decisive game, in which one side or the other—and by this we really assumed *our* side—always won. We went into Korea with our most recent victories still fresh in our minds, and that is one reason the war there was so frustrating.

Our Existence Was at Stake

We did not "win" in Korea. And we were disturbed when General [Douglas] MacArthur, with whom we associate so much of our previous military infallibility—and rightly so—warned, concerning Korea, that "there is no substitute for victory."

There *is* no substitute, of course, when one is engaged in an all-out, fight-or-die struggle, when the war is total and all the chips are down. Against the Germans and the Japanese, who were on the rampage and were playing for keeps, there could have been no substitute for victory. We were in those wars all the way; we had reached the finals, and the championship—our physical existence—was at stake. We *had* to win or die in the attempt.

We also went to war against Germany and Japan at a time when the rest of the world was as equally determined as we to stop them. Germany had made the mistake of taking on too much of the world at once. And hers was a blatant and arrogant mission: to Germanize the world. It was a useless, inexcusable mission. It did not even have the saving grace of claiming to forward a political idea. Unlike Russia—who tries, with some success, to camouflage her mission as a crusade to undo the economic wrongs of the world—Germany had nothing to offer the world except a disgusting display of racialism. The world was nauseated at the sight, and because it was a stronger world in those days and had not been bled white of its manpower and its will, it was not difficult to muster a concentrated alliance of power against the Nazis. Once Germany was ringed on all sides by powerful armies—and one glance at a map will show the difficulty, if not the impossibility, of repeating this tactic against the land mass of

China and Russia—she was finished.

The Japanese, the most industrialized and "modernized" nation of Asia, took us on in a similar match. Again the challenge was total and demanded a total response. We won again, because we were able to concentrate enough force to defeat an enemy who had challenged our very existence.

We were successful in both these wars because we were able to bring to bear a preponderance of power against two enemies who had staked everything they had. The U.S. started late, but because of our industrial genius we were able to outstrip both nations at once in the production of the guns, ships, planes, bullets, and bombs needed to bring them to their knees. And we took that immense gamble with our materials and our men because the crisis had reached its peak danger point. There were no preliminaries. Had we stopped the Japanese in Manchuria in 1931, or nipped Germany's mad mission in the bud when she entered the Sudetenland in 1938, we might have saved ourselves countless troubles and thousands of lives later on.

That, of course, is why we had to go to Korea. We had learned, against both Germany and Japan, whom we challenged only when the finals rolled around, that it is best, if only from a training standpoint, to get in on the preliminaries when we can. We learn the enemy's tactics that way, and we are better prepared to oppose him if he should choose to challenge us later in a showdown match.

Chipping Away at Our Resolve

Korea was a preliminary. The enemy, by his very choice of that tiny, insignificant country as a battleground, made it so. If he had wanted to defeat us, militarily, and take the championship title immediately, he would not have chosen Korea. He would have chosen, instead, to push his strength in industrial Germany or in some other more centrally located and more indispensable arena—perhaps even America—where we would have had to respond to him, as we did against Germany and Japan, with all our power. And he would have had to do the same. He would have had to summon all *his* resources and all *his* planes and armies in an attempt to crush us for good.

It is obvious that the enemy does not relish such a conflict. Instead, he has taken the expedient action of picking on us in little jabs, in small, isolated places like Korea and Indo-China [now known as Vietnam]—and perhaps more to come—where we cannot possibly come to grips with him. We have to respond, for he is clever enough to choose sensitive spots we cannot let go by default. But he knows when he starts the battle that it will not become a death trap for *him*. His only hope is that we will be sucked so far into a series of little wars and commit so much of our determination and strength in trying to "win" them that we will soon tire and collapse of our own exertion.

The Only Way to Win Is to Go Straight to the Source

We could no more defeat Communism in Korea than the enemy could defeat democracy there. It was too small a battleground on which to settle such a huge conflict. And we could no more have defeated Communism on the peninsula of Korea—just because we happened to be engaged there with some Communist forces—than we could have defeated Nazism down on the peninsula of Italy or the Japanese down in New Guinea. We had to enter Germany itself to cut out the roots of Nazism—the steel mills which supplied its armies and the people who blindly supported them. We had to lie off the shores of Japan, after tackling most of the stepping-stones in between, before she finally gave up. Similarly, if we are ever to attempt a final pitched battle against Communism, we shall have to bring to bear all the military power we have on Russia herself, and on Red China too. That is a formidable job even to think about. We are definitely not prepared for it yet. The fires are not that hot, and there are still enough alternatives to an all-consuming conflict that we can afford to hope, a little at least, that such a battle will never come off.

That is why we had to stop where and when we did in

Korea. There was no point in straining ourselves any further. We had accomplished the mission we assigned ourselves when we took on North Korea: we had stuck it out through three years of fantastically difficult and bloody warfare. We had proved we were willing to fight. But unless we *were* prepared for the finals, for an all-out war against Russia and China themselves, we were wasting whatever energy and power we continued to apply in Korea. As any experienced fighter knows, preliminaries are not supposed to be fifteen-round bouts, and for good reasons.

To have fought on in Korea would have been a little like trying to kill a lively and hostile octopus by hacking away at just one of its tentacles instead of at its brain. It might have been the braver and more impressive thing to do, to go on hacking away in Korea. But discretion in war, as in other endeavors, is the better part of valor. I have known a number of heroes who have won dozens of medals for their military exploits. But in most cases I have noticed that the hero, at the moment when he performed the brave and fearless act for which the world applauded him, was practically devoid of judgment and discretion. He was angry and in his anger he was willing to risk his life rather than live to fight another day. Heroes are the catalysts of warfare, and when a nation is in trouble it needs all the brave, foolhardy men it can find to man the bunkers and fly the riskier missions. And they deserve all the honors we can bestow on them. But if the nation *itself* becomes foolhardy, and in its frustration engages en masse in an unnecessary tampering with the odds, it may find itself carrying its valor indiscreetly close to the edge of suicide. Discretion is not only the better *part* of valor. According to [fifth-century B.C. Greek dramatist] Euripides, "Discretion *is* valor. A daring pilot is dangerous to his ship."

How to Defeat the Enemy

When President-elect [Dwight D.] Eisenhower arrived in Korea for his inspection trip, he spent three days visiting division and corps command posts, saw a demonstration of

ROK [Republic of Korea] training methods, and was briefed constantly by the generals who were in command of the war. Correspondents were not privileged to attend the President's private briefings, but from the facts that were generally known at the time, I have reconstructed the following outline of what the generals probably told him. I was briefed on most of these facts myself by one of General [Mark] Clark's highest staff officers:

1. We *could*, with enough men and supplies, push the enemy back to the Yalu [River].

2. Or, if that were considered unnecessary to our cause, we *could*, at least, inflict heavy damage on the enemy forces then in Korea.

3. We *could*, in order to accomplish this, break through the enemy's front line and chew up his forces. It would be a formidable task. And it would require a much larger force than we had in Korea at the time. During the long stalemate periods, when both sides had been trying to come to terms, the enemy had hedged his bet on peace and had so improved his positions that when Eisenhower visited Korea the enemy was dug in along the front in a solid interlocking series of fortifications twenty miles *in depth*. (Considering the cost, against massed enemy artillery and his unlimited manpower, of taking just one hill a thousand yards to our front, it is not difficult to imagine the problem of trying to penetrate twenty miles of enemy positions.) The generals told Eisenhower that to crack this line—which we would have to do if we were to attempt to roll back the enemy—would require sustaining an estimated 50,000 casualties.

4. Once we had broken through, we would need additional men, to replace those casualties and to beef up our units for the extensive job of mopping up and following our attack through to a final victory. We would have to keep moving north, of course, in order to keep the enemy on the run and prevent him from regrouping for a counterattack. We would take additional casualties during this operation, not so high, perhaps, as those required for breaching the line.

5. We might *not* be able to pull off another end run as successful as the operation MacArthur produced at Inchon. We caught the enemy off balance on that one, and unprepared. We had also taught *him* a lesson. As a result, he now had plenty of reserves scattered all the way from his front lines to the Yalu, organized and equipped to counter any attempt on our part to outflank him from the rear. We could *try* to pull off a landing but it might not be nearly so successful as Inchon, and certainly it would be expensive in lives.

6. In order to defeat the enemy *in Korea,* we would have to combine a concerted frontal attack, as outlined in Item 3, with a landing, as in Item 5. This, of course, would result in sustaining a *combination* of the casualties we would suffer in either operation. And at the same time we could expect the enemy to beef up his own forces with troops he had standing by in China. The war would not be won or over by any means.

7. We *could* try all this, however, the commanding generals told Eisenhower, if he but gave the word and provided the necessary men and supplies. (It should be pointed out here that generals are paid to fight, not to think up reasons for *avoiding* a fight. This was the only war we had, and it is natural that the generals in command of it, in Tokyo and Seoul, whose profession is warfare, should have thought in terms of continuing it. It might also be pointed out that President Eisenhower, who was once a commanding general himself, was familiar with this military psychology and undoubtedly took it into account.)

If the generals thought they had convinced him we should fight on, however, they were wrong. For when the President-elect flew home and had been inaugurated, he sent back word that the delegates at Panmunjom were to proceed with their endeavor to reach an armistice, and that they should make early arrangement to bring home the sick and wounded prisoners. He agreed, apparently, with Euripides. He would be a safe rather than a "daring" pilot. He would bring the Korean war to an honorable conclusion and husband our strength, our power, *and* our lives for some future and, he hoped, more advantageous time and place to apply them.

The Perfect Place to Draw Our Lines
The line we finally halted on is probably the best place in Korea for us to hole up. The so-called MacArthur Line, across the narrow waist of Korea, has received a great deal of publicity. And because it is shorter it is generally referred to as a better, cheaper line to maintain. However, it is one hundred miles farther north, and though this would give us one hundred extra miles of Korea with which to placate Syngman Rhee's ardent desire for unification, it would also give us an extra hundred miles of severe military headaches.

Had we pushed the enemy farther north, we would have done so at the cost of giving him an advantage and ourselves a disadvantage. For one thing, we would have extended our own supply line by a hundred miles. We would have had to haul our rations, our ammunition stocks, and our new men an extra hundred miles beyond where we now have to haul them to get them to our defensive positions. And at the same time we would have *shortened* the enemy's supply lines for *him*. He would have one hundred less miles of roads and railroads over which he had to supply his troops. Moving north, then, would have made our job more difficult and his a good deal easier. And we would have sustained the afore-mentioned losses just pushing our line up in the first place. There did not seem to be much point in that. We would also be stuck, as a result, with the responsibility of occupying some ten thousand square miles of territory which the enemy had held before and which we had wrecked with our bombs. To prevent civil unrest, disease, and economic chaos we would have been obliged to rebuild it all ourselves. There would not have been much point in taking on that extra chore either.

In addition to all this, we would have placed ourselves one hundred miles nearer the enemy's sanctuary across the Yalu. We would be that much closer to his MIG bases, and thus in greater danger of air attack should the war be resumed.

We are sitting now on a line that is reasonably safe from attack by the enemy's MIGs. The MIG, like all jets, is a high-altitude plane. It performs efficiently in the rarefied atmosphere of twenty or thirty thousand feet, and it uses minimum fuel at a high altitude. But once it descends—and a plane would have to come down on the deck, of course, to an altitude of a few hundred feet to strafe or bomb ground troops—it begins to burn fuel so fast, because of the higher oxygen content at that level, that its range is cut down tremendously. Where we sit now, manning our wall against Communism, the MIG cannot come down, attack our positions, and have enough fuel left over to return safely to its bases on the Yalu. We are just out of reach. Had we gone farther north we would have lessened that advantage. There would not have been much point in that. . . .

We shall not be able to relax. And we shall have to keep our men in Korea for a long time to come, dug in along the front and ready for action. But the price for our alertness will not be so high. The men will be able to fly to Tokyo a little oftener to drink the good Japanese beer and buy gay kimonos for their girl friends. They will also be able to stand up in the noonday sun in Korea and strip down to their white T-shirts or to their bare skin without worrying about the enemy's using their unarmored bodies for target practice. They will not be content, and their parents at home will worry about them and wonder why they should have to sit out in Korea at all when the war there is over. But they will be alive. They at least will not be sitting in some crowded enemy prison camp or lie buried in the U.N. cemetery at Pusan. And they will be serving a good and necessary purpose. Japan and Korea will be safe. We will have two footholds in Asia which we would not have if we had defaulted in June 1951. There will be two less places we would have to take back for our own protection, at some future and deadlier date, when the price would have been even higher.

We will have our wall.

The Korean Conflict Changed the Way the United States Fights Wars

Matthew B. Ridgway

General Matthew B. Ridgway had commanded the Eighty-second Airborne Division during World War II as well as the Eighth Army in Korea. He eventually took over command of all UN forces in Korea from General Douglas MacArthur, who had been relieved of his command by President Harry S. Truman. The following excerpt is from Ridgway's autobiography, which was released at the beginning of the U.S. entry into the Vietnam War. Ridgway compares the Korean War and the Vietnam War, both of which signaled an end to the large, set-piece battles of the past. He states there is a need for new objectives in the nuclear age. This viewpoint of a limited war differed from General MacArthur's more traditional mode of thinking, which sought only total victory at any cost.

There would be little purpose in dwelling at length on the lessons taught us by wars of the past if we did not endeavor seriously to apply those lessons to the military problems of today. Above all, I believe we need to read the lessons closely lest we repeat, at inestimable cost, the mistakes for which we paid so dear a price.

One of the major mistakes of Korea was our tendency to try to base our strategy on a reading of enemy intentions, while failing to give proper weight to what we knew of enemy capabilities. MacArthur and those who supported him belittled the Chinese threat to intervene in Korea, even though they knew that Red China was perfectly capable of carrying out that threat promptly. But we based our moves on the theory that "no commander in his right mind" would commit his forces south of the Yalu [River, which runs between North Korea and China,] at that time.

Today, as we grapple with our mounting difficulties in Southeast Asia, it is satisfying to note that we seem to concern ourselves more with what we *know* the enemy is capable of and less with what we *think* he is planning. President [Lyndon B.] Johnson has said that he takes Red China at her word—something we failed to do in Korea. I have no doubt, therefore, that our planners are well aware that the Red Chinese are capable, if their leaders so decide, of provoking us into a war with them. Their public statements have already made it clear that their regard for human lives, even of their own citizens, bears little resemblance to ours. While I am not privy to current plans, I feel confident that we are preparing to meet the exercise of Red China's most dangerous capability. I am uneasy only when I hear influential voices assuring us that China "would not dare" make this move or that, and I trust that our military planners will never again be lulled by faulty reading of the Communist Chinese mind.

Failing to Learn from Our Mistakes

Still, even though we may have learned that one lesson well, there are other mistakes that at least a portion of our citizenry seems bent on repeating. There were those who felt, at the time of the Korean War, that air power might accomplish miracles of interdiction, by cutting all the flow of reinforcement and supply to the embattled enemy. The fact that it could not accomplish these miracles has not yet been accepted as widely as it should have been. No one who fought on the ground in Korea would ever be tempted to belittle the accomplishments of our air force there. Not only did air power save us from disaster, but without it the mission of the United Nations Forces could not have been accomplished. In Vietnam too it has made all the difference between success on the ground and frustration. But air power does have its definite limitations, and even some in high position still fail to acknowledge them.

These limitations were never better illustrated than in World War II, when the Germans were able to maintain some twenty-six divisions south of the Alps in Italy, using a few mountain passes to keep them supplied for two years, regardless of uncontested Allied air supremacy. In Korea, where we had air mastery over practically the whole peninsula, MacArthur himself acknowledged our inability to isolate the battle area by air bombardment or to choke off the flow of reinforcements and supply. In Vietnam, results to date have repeated this lesson: rails and bridges are repaired and functioning within a few days of a bomb attack, and infiltration routes have not been cut off. Yet we still hear calls for saturation bombing that will, its proponents insist, cut off North Vietnam from the south.

I am doubtful too if we have learned from Korea the further lesson that agreements with the Communists are of no account unless ironclad sanctions which can and will be enforced are included. Two years of trying negotiations in Korea taught us that Communists will fulfill agreements only when it is to their clear advantage to do so or when the threat of retaliation is too clear to be ignored. Whatever settlement is finally reached with the Communists in Southeast Asia, the inclusion of enforceable sanctions is bound to present extreme difficulties. We must be prepared, however, to face up to the necessity of postponing final agreement until such sanctions have been settled on.

Understanding the Limited War

One mistake we avoided in Korea was an insistence on "total victory" or "unconditional surrender" or even a "halt to aggression" before talking peace. But in the light of many of the slogans that fill the air and the public prints nowadays, I am moved to wonder if all our citizens have come to understand the concept of limited war. A limited war is not merely a small war that has not yet grown to full size. It is a war in which the objectives are specifically limited in the light of our national interest and our current capabilities. A war that is "open-ended"—that has no clearly delineated geographical, political, and military goals beyond "victory"—is a war that may escalate itself indefinitely, as wars will, with one success requiring still another to insure the first one. An insistence on going all-out to win a war may have a fine masculine ring, and a call to "defend freedom" may have a messianic sound that stirs our blood. But the ending of an all-out war in these times is beyond imagining. It may mean the turning back of civilization by several thousand years, with no one left capable of signaling the victory.

War Is Not the Only Recourse

In setting our military goals we need first of all to recognize that most of the world's most basic woes do not lend themselves to purely military solutions. In our clashes with ideologies that deride the dignity of man and deny him his individual freedom, solutions must be sought through combined political, economic, and military efforts. The world is not likely to settle into equilibrium while less than one-third of its population lives on a plateau of comparative luxury and the other two-thirds knows only poverty, squalor, and want.

The objectives of our foreign policy, therefore, must take these basic realities into account and must be stated clearly enough so they cannot become mere war cries behind which we conceal selfish and materialistic aims. I have considerable doubt, for instance, that the objectives of our Vietnam war effort, as articulated by certain government officials, mean exactly what they say, even granting the plain fact that diplomacy can seldom deal in truth, or seldom in truth complete and unadorned. President Johnson's stated objectives, as of this writing (January 1967), seem to me clear of ambiguity and hidden meaning, and about as far as our government can go with honor and without appeasement. But the pleadings of others in official or influential position that our war aims in Vietnam are wholly altruistic and bent merely on guaranteeing to the people there the "freedom to choose their own government" strike me as open to question. It was not too long ago that President [Dwight D.] Eisenhower equated the loss of Vietnam with the "loss of valuable deposits of tin and prodigious supplies of rubber and rice." Perhaps one may be allowed to suspect that these commodities, rather than "freedom," are the real prize that certain eyes are fastened on. And those who state our aim as being "to cause Hanoi [North Vietnam] to cease aggression" ignore the fact that Hanoi's effort could not long continue without support and supply from Peking [China].

An Ultimatum Would Be Ineffective

If we were to place credence in that latter statement of our objective, we would in effect be saying that our aim is to force both Hanoi *and* Peking to cease their support of armed aggression and subversion, not only against Vietnam but against Laos, Cambodia, Thailand, and Burma, to all of which the United States has commitments under the Southeast Asia Treaty. And logic then would dictate that the United States should, either openly or through secret diplomatic channels, convey an ultimatum to Communist China to cease and desist. For myself, I have grave doubts of the wisdom of any course that would involve an ultimatum to the Red Chinese. The present Chinese leaders would, I believe, spurn any ultimatum, by whatever means it might be conveyed to them. If we should be obliged to extend our military operations to thwart aggression aimed at the overthrow of the other states in Southeast Asia, under the aegis of the Southeast Asia Treaty, I believe we would find it necessary greatly to increase our troop commitment there. And, in my opinion, whatever overall strength we might feel justified in committing there would still prove insufficient without the tactical use of nuclear weapons, the consequences of which can only be surmised.

Finally, I believe the use of nuclear weapons against industrial and population centers—unless an enemy uses them first against our territory or forces—would so revolt free world opinion as to leave us, quite possibly, friendless and isolated in a hostile world.

It behooves us therefore to decide among ourselves what the objectives of our world policy should be—to define them with care and to make sure they lie within the range of our vital national interests and that their accomplishment is within our capabilities. Our resources are not endless, and to expend them all in the pursuit of vague and unreachable objectives might render us unable to meet the ultimate test that, I feel, is surely on its way. . . .

Our Vital Interests

Our general world objectives—those that clearly lie within the zone of our vital national interests—are more open to debate. But some, I believe, are clearly definable. These include, but are not limited to, the following:

1. To prevent Western Europe, outside the Iron Curtain, from coming under Kremlin [Soviet] control.

2. To prevent the establishment of a Kremlin-dominated government in the Western Hemisphere (an objective temporarily lost sight of with respect to Cuba, but still an objective).

3. To maintain our forward defense line in the Far East, i.e., the line of the Japanese Islands—South Korea—the Ryukyus—Formosa—the Philippines. (Whether all or part of Southeast Asia is to be included is, in my judgment, a debatable point.)

4. To continue support of the United Nations under the principles of its charter, particularly with regard to the promise of the charter preamble: "To save succeeding generations from the scourge of war. . . ."

(Many Americans may disagree with the inclusion of that point as an objective within the zone of our vital interests. But so be it.)

By my way of thinking, to save our children, and their

children, from the scourge of war lies within the sphere of vital interests, not only of the American people, but of the people of the whole world. And starting a war—deliberately provoking a nuclear war, for example—is not the way to save them. Indeed that phrase from the preamble seems to me to set forth the most vital aim of the United Nations.

From the time of Rome's greatness until now—a period of two millennia—the peoples of Europe have been periodically deluged in blood by wars which, within the last two centuries, have grown increasingly murderous and have laid wider areas to waste. Now, with the existing potential for destruction, a new world war would charge a price in blood and in annihilation of human values that would be past all reckoning.

An All-Out War Needs to Be Avoided at All Costs

In the very ghastliness of this possible catastrophe should lie the hope that the sanity and wisdom of statesmen will devise ways to prevent it. No present obstacle, no foreseeable difficulty—certainly not human greed and lust for power—should be permitted to defeat or weaken collective efforts to stave off the unthinkable. No group of nations has greater stakes at issue, or stronger reasons—apart from the inherent moral imperative—for attaining this objective than do the peoples of Western Europe and America—Europe, because of its long history of death and devastation by war; America, because of the identity of its cultural and economic interests with those of Europe, and both together because of the extreme vulnerability of their highly developed social, economic, and cultural structures. . . .

I believe firmly that our Western civilization evolved on this planet in accordance with some high, though inscrutable, purpose. This purpose, I believe, does not cast the American nation in the role of Messiah among the less fortunate peoples of the earth, but rather in the role of strong, courageous, and broad-minded associates, fully aware of our own limitations, conscious of our own capabilities, and devoid of any desire to force our institutions and our way of life on others. Our material as well as our spiritual strength is sufficient to fulfill this high purpose, provided only that we develop the wisdom to accept our role.

For the present I believe there is no higher duty than the preservation of our freedom. That requires us to husband our strength, not squander it, for use when we face the supreme test. But the mere statement of a purpose is valueless. It must be translated into concrete and pragmatic political objectives that, as I have noted before, should conform to our vital national interests and be subordinated to them.

I am frankly doubtful that we are, in Southeast Asia, setting our objectives within this frame. A citizen outside the flow of high-level governmental intelligence, as I am, cannot of course resolve that doubt with any certainty. Yet, under our form of government, it is every citizen's duty to attempt, on the basis of what he is permitted to know, to evaluate the foreign-policy problems that face us, to utter his honest views, and to be mindful of the many erroneous assessments of the Southeast Asia problem that have been pronounced from Washington in the recent past.

While I am, as I said, not at all convinced that our political objectives in Southeast Asia—manifold, tenuous, and imprecise as have been those set forth by our government officials—really harmonize with our national interests, I do not believe that these misstatements should be our primary concern. Rather we should ask ourselves now if we are not, in this open-ended conflict, so impairing our strength through overdrawing on our resources—political, economic, and military—as to find ourselves unduly weakened when we need to meet new challenges in other more vital areas of the world. For there surely will be threats that bear more closely on our true national interests.

If we find the wisdom to husband our strength against the day when those threats appear, then I am utterly confident in America's future, in the capacity of our leadership to meet those threats, and in the ability of our armed forces to contribute in full measure to that leadership.

3

WE WERE THERE: A PERSONAL PERSPECTIVE OF KOREA

We Are Fighting Against Imperialism: The North Korean Perspective

International Public Opinion Research, Inc.

During the Korean War, Johns Hopkins University hired a research firm, International Public Opinion Research, Inc., to interview 768 North Korean and 238 Chinese prisoners of war (POWs) who were being held in camps in Korea during the winter of 1950–1951. The purpose of these interviews was to determine the extent of the prisoners' Communist indoctrination as well as the effectiveness of the psychological warfare tactics employed by the United States against North Korea. Questions asked included what the POWs thought was the cause of the war and what they thought about the United States and its allies. Most of the North Korean prisoners believed that South Korea had instigated the invasion, and the Chinese POWs believed that they were protecting their country from a U.S. invasion. The following excerpt is taken from the resulting one-hundred-ten-page report and quotes prisoner responses to questions.

The purpose of these reports is (a) to determine as far as possible the effect upon the enemy of current psychological warfare operations, particularly propaganda leaflets, (b) to identify and solve methodological problems encountered in the course of pursuing the above goal, and (c) to make recommendations for increasing the effectiveness of future psychological warfare.

The two memoranda submitted previously discussed the

International Public Opinion Research, Inc., *Belief of Enemy Soldiers About the Korean War*. Chevy Chase, MD: Operations Research Office, Johns Hopkins University, 1952. Copyright © 1952 by Johns Hopkins University. Reproduced by permission.

influence of current psychological warfare operations on the capture-surrender behavior of North Korean and Chinese Communist prisoners of war, in the light of certain other immediate and direct influences on behavior: the military situation, expectations about prisoner treatment, length of military service, and other background factors. The present report is peripheral to the main purposes of the series in that the material with which it deals is not so directly related to capture-surrender behavior as that summarized in the other reports. It fixes attention on what the prisoners knew of political affairs, and the extent to which they were Communist-indoctrinated. . . .

The interviews made little attempt to elicit prisoner opinion on matters not directly related to psychological warfare or to their own military experience. This limitation was imposed in view of the serious difficulties that must be surmounted in order to get reliable answers to questions calculated to obtain expressions of opinion rather than of information. For example, the prisoners had a natural desire to show that they were not Communists and that they considered Americans fine people. Thus certain questions that had proved useful in international public opinion research in the past were not used, because of the danger that the answers would be unreliable.

Conceivably, of course, many prisoners actually do prefer western democracy to communism. In order to arrive at a reliable estimate of how many, however, it would be necessary to obtain long and careful interviews, based on adequate experiment and pretesting, and conducted by extremely skilled interviewers with (preferably) some background in social science. The deadline for the present study precluded this kind of interviewing, and it was decided that the principal aims of the study—the evaluation of psychological warfare—could be achieved without reliable data on the prisoners' opinions about democracy and communism.

Some of the questions used to obtain the data for this report were "loaded" questions, and unreliable answers were to be expected. Often, however, unreliable content can be detected, and the unreliable part of an answer ignored. For instance, many answers to the question about how the war started read, "I thought that South Korea started the war, but now I know that it isn't true." The latter part of such an answer may well be unreliable, but it can be disregarded without prejudice to the earlier part, which provides information as to the state of mind of enemy soldiers in general.

Sample Selected
A total of 1,006 prisoners were interviewed during the field work phase of this study. Interviewing started on 31 December 1950 and ended on 5 March 1951, during which time interviewers talked with 768 North Korean and 238 Chinese prisoners. Most of the Chinese and a little less than half of the North Koreans were interviewed within two days to two weeks of their capture by, or surrender to, UN troops. The others had been in the hands of the UN forces for varying periods, ranging up to several months, at the time of interview.

Personnel
Interviewing was accomplished by a staff of 15 native Koreans, five of whom were fluent in at least one Chinese dialect. The interviews were recorded in Korean, and subsequently rendered into English by a staff of 19 translators.

Indoctrination of Enemy Soldiers
All the prisoners in the sample were asked what they had been told about the US, about Russia, about the UN, and about South Korea (the Chinese were asked about both South Korea and North Korea). The information they reported does not necessarily reflect what the prisoners actually believed about these countries. It does reveal what the Communist leaders evidently want their troops to believe about their friends and enemies. And it should help to provide a clearer picture of the enemy's domestic propaganda, which our psywar [psychological warfare] activities must be designed to combat. . . .

Both North Korean and Chinese leaders had apparently attempted to justify the war with the US by portraying it as a dangerous enemy to their people. They had not, however, made use of identical specific charges against the US.

The North Korean propagandists had stressed alleged plans on the part of the US to take Korea over as a colony. When the North Korean prisoners repeated this accusation, they usually coupled it with another frequent allegation—that the US was planning further aggression:

"[The United States] is interfering by force in order to make Korea her colony. She intends to make Korea a military base for the invasion of China and Russia." (POW #793)

"The United States is training the South Korean army for the purpose of invading North Korea. Under the guise of economic assistance the US takes away the natural resources of Korea and sends them to America. The US is going to make Korea a colony and use it for a military base when it invades Russia." (POW #407)

The designs of the US on Korea had, the responses show, often been described as fitting into an alleged pattern of imperialistic behavior involving numerous potential "victims":

"The US is an imperialistic country which is trying to make all the small, weak nations of the world her colonies. She is trying to make Korea her colony too. She takes valuable materials out of Korea and brings in useless articles. She wants to occupy Korea because Korea would be an important military base in a fight against China and Russia." (POW #632)

Sometimes the broad pattern of imperialism had been alleged without specific application to Korea:

"America provoked war in order to colonize small

countries and control the whole world. She sells her goods and enslaves many people. . . ." (POW #645)

Comments stressing the allegedly imperialistic behavior of the US had frequently been accompanied by criticism of the US on the grounds that it is a capitalist nation. Internal economic difficulties arising out of capitalism had usually been cited as reasons for America's "invasion" of the small, weak nations of the world:

> "The US is controlled by capitalists. It is not true that the US is helping Korea to bring about the independence of Korea. The US is an imperialist and capitalist nation, which is trying to take advantage of Korea under the pretext of helping Korea to win independence. The US is facing an economic crisis as a result of overproduction, and in order to avoid this crisis she is making war on small weak nations." (POW #418)

> "The US is a highly developed capitalist state, and there are many unemployed persons because of a financial panic. The government exports surplus materials to foreign countries, and adopts this as an instrument for invading the nations of the world." (POW #625)

References, like that above (to the condition of the American people under capitalism), had been infrequent. When the leaders had mentioned the people of the US at all, they had done so in terms of suffering from unemployment or some other alleged form of capitalistic exploitation, and fierce popular opposition to the fighting in Korea:

> "There is much unemployment in the US. Even now there are frequent strikes in opposition to this war. The US will come to internal destruction in the near future." (POW #649)

To judge from the comments of the CCF [Chinese Communist forces] prisoners, the Chinese leaders had been even more extreme than the North Koreans in castigating the US for alleged aggressiveness and war-mongering. Sometimes their accusations had been of a highly generalized character:

"They said that the US was a capitalistic and aggressive country and was going to dominate the world." (POW #1102)

Usually, however, US enmity toward China and US designs for conquest had been mentioned specifically, and reference had often been made to a desire on the part of the US to help Chiang Kai-shek [leader of the Chinese Nationalist government, who was exiled to Taiwan,] regain his authority:

"The US is an aggressive nation. She wants to invade China and re-establish Chiang Kai-shek's political powers in China, to oppress the people." (POW #1138)

"At present, America is controlling South Korea. In the future, she will invade China in order to get our abundant underground resources." (POW #1002)

The implicit charge of imperialism in the above statement had been made more explicit in some of the anti-US remarks recalled by prisoners. Sometimes the charge had been urged in vague, general terms like the following:

"The US is an imperialistic nation. It instigates the weaker nations into making war and losing the lives of many innocent people." (POW #1110)

More often, however, it had been combined with the charge of aggressive intentions:

"The US is an imperialistic nation, and after she invades North Korea she will attack China. Therefore, she is helping Chiang Kai-shek, to enable the Central Army to return to the Chinese mainland." (POW #1117)

"America is an imperialist country and she is aggressive. Having agitated all the minor countries of the world she is gathering them under her control. She has given arms to Japan and Western Germany. She is eagerly seeking a chance to invade China." (POW #1127) . . .

In general, the North Korean leaders' comments, as revealed by the prisoners, had reflected the hostility of a small nation afraid of being overrun by an enemy: two-thirds of the prisoners repeated accusations that the US aims to reduce Korea to a colony in order to make it into a market for its goods; one out of four remembers more general allegations of imperialism on the part of the US; and four out of ten said they had heard the US branded as an aggressor or warmonger.

The Chinese leaders' comments, by contrast, had reflected the hostility of a nation that deems itself the peer of the country with which it is at odds. The alleged danger of invasion had been expressed, but not the fear of being overrun. The Chinese leaders had been highly specific as to why the US was an enemy: two-thirds of the Chinese soldiers repeated the accusation that the US was against the People's Government of their country, was helping its enemies, or planning an invasion; and almost as many (for the most part the same prisoners) said that the US had been denounced on numerous occasions as an aggressor and warmonger. Only one out of three CCF prisoners recalled generalized accusations of imperialism, while a slightly smaller proportion of North Koreans remembered such accusations. . . .

What POWs Had Been Told About Russia

Almost all the North Koreans and most of the Chinese stated that their leaders had spoken to them about Russia. Of the better educated North Koreans, for example, 99 percent answered the question on this point affirmatively. . . .

What the North Koreans had been told about Russia dif-

fered little from what the Chinese had been told. Both groups had heard Russia described most frequently as their country's liberator and ally, and the source of assistance of various kinds:
Chinese POWs:

> "They said that Russia was our big brother. It had helped China during World War II. It had liberated China from the bondage of the Japanese. Red China was depending on Russia in every way for the reconstruction of China." (POW #1131)

> "Russia is China's big brother. Russia is giving tremendous help in order to reconstruct the factories and railroads of China which had been destroyed by Chiang Kai-shek's Army." (POW #1138)

A North Korean POW:

> "Russia liberated Korea from the yoke of the Japanese. She is helping Korea to develop in a democratic fashion. She brings machines for the factories and sends teachers to explain new techniques. She will improve farming by bringing tractors to the farmers." (POW #627)

The above is typical of a large number of the reports of discussion of Russia by North Korean leaders. In a large number of other cases, Russia's assistance to Korea had been presented as an aspect of her friendship for all small, weak nations:

> "Russia liberated weak and small nations and helped them toward self-government. For the North Korean government she provides instructors in military tactics, and supplies arms, and politically she is helping to put a democratic plan into effect. This is true assistance and Russia has no territorial ambitions." (POW #605)

It is interesting to notice that the Korean leaders, in their statements about Russia's friendship for Korea, had often insisted that Russia keeps out of Korea's internal affairs—that, for example, Russia had withdrawn her troops, which had not returned even when the war started:

> "The Russians withdrew from Korea for the sake of Korea's independence. But the US does not withdraw because she wants to make South Korea into a colony. Russia has no desire to colonize weaker nations, but helps them. Russia liberated North Korea." (POW #623)

> "North Korea should try to develop good will between itself and Russia, just as though they were brothers. Generalissimo [Joseph] Stalin liberated Korea and helped us so that Koreans can lead better lives. Russia did not participate in this war, saying, 'The troubles in Korea should be settled by the Koreans themselves.'" (POW #637)

In Enemy Hands: An American POW's Perspective

Larry Zellers

Larry Zellers was an American teacher and missionary who worked in Kaesong when it was part of South Korea. Kaesong was captured and recaptured throughout the war, eventually becoming part of North Korea. Kaesong was located near the thirty-eighth parallel and was one of the first cities attacked by North Korea. Zellers and a group of missionaries, foreign diplomats, journalists, and American soldiers had been captured and subjected to constant interrogation and Communist indoctrination. The following excerpt from Zellers's autobiography illustrates the methods the Communists used to try to subvert his will and get him to denounce his own country and ideals. It also reveals how differing ideologies between individuals and nations can lead to conflict.

There were many interrogators working on me, each with a different tactic. I have no idea where they got their training—certainly not from the Japanese. They appeared to use techniques against me that were very similar to those of the Chinese Communists, techniques intended to achieve the genuine reeducation of a prisoner's political views: hence their frequent advice to me to purge my old capitalistic thoughts and "have a clear conscience." To the North Koreans, a clear conscience meant correct political thinking.

My views about the intense psychological pressures that

Larry Zellers, *In Enemy Hands: A Prisoner in North Korea*. Lexington: University Press of Kentucky, 1991. Copyright © 1991 by the University Press of Kentucky. Reproduced by permission.

I endured in prison are similar to those of journalist Philip Deane. When asked after his release from North Korea whether he had been physically tortured, Deane gave a searching response: "Not in the strict sense of the word. The theory—and I learned the theory after I came out of prison—is that they act on the mind of the prisoner by exploiting fears he already has or implanting other fears. They confront the prisoner with these fears day and night, till he breaks."

With the exception of the controlled sinister climate that caused me at times to fear living more than dying—the sensory deprivation, the interrogations, the chronic fatigue that was just as bad on waking up in the morning as at night—I was not subjected to what we usually consider torture. I don't know why. If they had used torture on me, they would have won whatever they wanted; I have no doubt about that.

My next interrogator, one I had never seen before, apparently worked alone.

"Rarry [Larry], where is your pistol? We didn't find one when we arrested you."

"I don't have one."

"You teach ideology in your house in Kaesong."

"I sometimes discuss religion in my house." I was being careful in my answers.

"Then you admit that you teach ideology in your house?" he pressed on.

"I teach a class in modern literature once each week in my house. Some of that literature discusses Christianity. I suppose from your point of view I do teach ideology, but attendance is strictly voluntary."

"You are hiding something. You admit that you teach ideology and yet you do not have a pistol."

"I don't need a pistol. Everyone is permitted to come to my house if he wishes. They are not required to attend." He appeared to be agitated by my answers.

"Do you believe in what you teach?" he demanded.

"Yes, very much."

"If you really believed in what you taught, you would have a pistol, and everyone would be required to listen."

"Does everyone in your country believe in your ideology?" I asked, thinking I might divert him from the subject.

"No, some do not, but they are poisoned by capitalistic thoughts. In any case, they do not matter. But they will at least know our ideology. We require them to know it. You do not require it of your people. You are not sincere."

My interrogator seemed to be a very excitable person and a chain smoker. His questions indicated to me that he had his own agenda. I had never seen him before, and I was never to see him again.

"How can you say that I am not sincere? Do you mean that I am lying?"

"Not necessarily. But if you really thought that your ideology was very important, you would have a pistol, and you would make people listen. Perhaps not all of them would believe you, but at least they would know about your teaching. You are not sincere!"

"Our system believes in tolerance," I replied, thinking that I was on safe ground.

"Tolerance! Ah! It is not tolerance at all. It is lack of conviction!" I could see the problem. In the eyes of the interrogators, either I did not carry a personal weapon, which they could not understand, or else I did carry one and they could not find it, which made them angry with me. There was a pause, and I thought about the general drift of our conversation. I had displayed one of our best ideological weapons, tolerance, and the interrogator regarded it as a sign of weakness.

A Question of Doctrine

My next interrogators, a set of three, attacked from still another direction, asking, "How much money did your parents earn per year?" My parents were rather poor farmers, so I had already surmised what the reaction would be to my answer.

"You lie!" they shouted. I soon realized the nature of the

problem. It was a question of doctrine. If my parents were poor, then how was I able to attend college? According to their little book, the children of parents who made less than a certain income were not able to go on to higher education. They were obviously faced with a conflict between their ideology and my testimony, and it had to be resolved.

I didn't know what else to do, so I remained silent as my interrogators shouted at me. I realized my plight early in that interrogation. Fact and fantasy alike must be bent to fit the prearranged plan. On certain issues, at least, it really didn't matter what I told them. It was obvious that these particular interrogators were more bureaucratic than the others. They would simply fill in the blanks, in as much detail as they chose, based upon the requirements of their plan. There had to be a way out of this dilemma for them, and there was.

"We will write in our report that your father was a wealthy landowner," one of them said at last, after much consultation with the other two. (My father had a good laugh when I told him about this on my return to America.)

I was beginning to feel like the unwilling participant in an ancient Greek tragedy, where the issues are already decided and the players merely going through the motions, playing out their appointed roles with as much grace, courage, and nobility as possible. With their roles already prescribed, the main characters win or lose, not by whether or not they live (they always die) but by how faithfully they play out their roles to the predictable end. Not a very noble way to make my exit, I thought.

They changed the subject again about that time. "When the peace-loving peoples of the world liberate the earth from capitalism, there will finally be peace." They could become positively misty-eyed when they talked like that. "You are a reactionary who is delaying that wonderful time when all of this takes place. Don't you feel ashamed of your actions?"

"I want you to know," I said, thinking I might make a point, "that I do not consider you to be my enemy." They were ready with an answer. "You may not consider us to be your enemy, but we know that you are ours." I wondered how my sociology teacher in college would have responded to that statement.

There Were No Right Answers
Then they returned to a matter that I had been dreading in a way but one that I wanted to know about: that tantalizing offer of hope. "Have you been thinking about what we asked you?"

"What did you ask me?" I reacted cautiously.

"We told you that you could have a happy future, remember?"

"Yes, I remember."

"Well, what about it? Do you want a happy future or not?" I knew that I was in a tight spot, no matter what I answered. It was dangerous to play along with them. From their point of view, there was no polite or acceptable way to turn them down without making them angry; after all, they were the teachers.

"I'm sorry," I replied at last. The three of them became very angry.

"Who do you think you are? Do you think that you are in a position to make bargains with us? You who are about to die?" One of them spat on the floor in apparent disgust as the other two raved on simultaneously.

"We have tried to save your life, but we can see that you don't appreciate it!" They appeared to be offended by my apparent ingratitude.

"My life isn't worth very much to me now anyway."

"Oh, you are complaining about your treatment! Please pay attention: unless you show us in some way that you are trying to change your thoughts and your conduct, you are not worthy of the kind of treatment you are now getting. You should try to be more grateful."

"What is it that I am not doing right?" I asked.

"You must change your attitude and submit to self-criticism. Your thinking is bad. You are poisoned with reactionary thinking."

When at last there was quiet, they all expected me to continue the conversation. I realized that anything I said or asked would be viewed as weakness, so I remained silent.

"Is that all you have to say?"

"Yes," I replied.

"If you continue to do as you are now doing, you will die. You will die soon."

Apparently, they felt that they had made their point and ushered me out of the room to be returned to my cell. When I walked by an adjoining room, my interrogator from the day before poked his head out the door and shouted after me. "You can have a happy future. Many nice things." His voice trailed off in singsong. I did not even look back. I preferred the death cell and the fleas. It was difficult to decide whether these men were more frightening when they appeared friendly or when they were openly hostile.

Dangling Carrots

My mind was very confused that night. I wondered why each set of interrogators seemed to pursue a different approach, yet all were aimed at breaking me down. Confusion reigned between their methods, but it could not be termed random confusion; it all had a purpose.

But I was becoming more and more enticed by the prospect of hope that the interrogators seemed to be offering me. Was there really a way out for me after all? Could I escape execution without betraying my country or compromising my beliefs? The peace of mind I had previously enjoyed was predicated upon Dr. [Ernst] Kisch's belief that our fate had already been decided before we were ever placed in the death cell, that nothing we said or did during our interrogations would make any difference concerning whether we lived or died. [Dr. Kisch, an Austrian missionary, was also a prisoner.]

Yet the interrogators at that time were certainly leading me to believe that I could save my life by something I might say. This belief would place a very high premium on how I conducted myself during those interrogations. Little by little, I was beginning to doubt what Dr. Kisch had said. To that same degree, I was becoming more troubled about my conduct during interrogations. Also, to that same degree, I was growing increasingly vulnerable to all the other stresses in that prison.

After a very miserable night in my cell, I was brought into a room to face three new interrogators. "We have been looking over your life history. Very interesting," one of them said with a smile. They always told me that no matter what I wrote.

"We noticed that you did not tell us who your fourth grade teacher was. What was her name?" I paused for a moment, thinking he might be joking. The speaker and the other interrogators sat very still, looking intently at me without saying a word. They were not joking.

"I'm sorry, I don't remember who my fourth grade teacher was," I replied, not even trying to hide my exasperation.

"Rarry, I thought you would know by now how important it is for you to cooperate with us. You seem to remember many other things. Why do you not remember this teacher?"

"I'm sorry, if I knew I would tell you."

"You are showing initiative, Rarry, and that is a very bad thing for anyone in your position to do!"

That word, "initiative" had a habit of creeping into their vocabulary quite often. I didn't know the Korean word for initiative. Inasmuch as English was used in all interrogations, I thought at first that the confusion might have resulted from a mistranslation of a Korean word into English. But the same English word would show up at odd times during the entire three years. Even on the Death March that was to follow, the one catch phrase that the North Koreans shouted up and down the line of marching men and women was, "Don't show initiative!"

It was impossible to convince the three interrogators that I was unable to follow their instructions. "I am sorry that I still cannot remember the name of my fourth grade teacher."

They were very unhappy with my answer. Immediately they launched into a tirade against me and everything I stood for. They made it very clear that I would have to answer for not cooperating. Their punishment was to interrogate me longer and more often. Finally, as they were returning me to my cell, they called after me, "If you didn't show initiative, things would be better for you!"....

Twisting the Facts

The same three people were waiting for me at my next interrogation. "Rarry, who started the war?" I had been worried that they would eventually ask me that question. Their lectures still claimed that South Korea began the war by attacking across the 38th parallel on June 24, 1950, and that they (the North Koreans) had counterattacked on June 25. As an eyewitness, I knew that view was false.

"I think North Korea started the war," I said, not knowing what they would do.

"You are lying, Rarry," one of them said in a calm voice. "South Korea started the war on June 24 and we counterattacked on June 25. You are showing initiative again, Rarry. You still do not understand. We will have to teach you." When I did not respond, the three of them launched into another long-winded harangue against me and every value known in the free world. At long last they had me returned to my cell.

With the passing of time in that death cell, another consideration besides that of mere survival began to surface. I decided not to carry any more excess baggage with me to my execution than absolutely necessary. I chose not to hate my captors. Much later, without the stimulation of impending execution, that old emotion would return on occasion, and dealing with it was difficult. But in that death cell, giving up hate was not difficult to do because it was too much of a burden.

Their little games continued every day that I spent in the death cell. I was never left alone for very long. Several times a day a "thought control" guard would test what was going on inside my mind. Throwing open the door of the cell, he would suddenly appear without warning. Jumping directly in front of me and pointing his finger in my face, he would scream, "What are you thinking about?" I'd usually respond that I was thinking about home and loved ones.

"*Napan sangok*—bad thoughts! You should be thinking about your many crimes against the people!" I was never punished for my "bad thoughts" except by screaming lectures, but I always dreaded the verbal examination.

The stress was beginning to make me feel numb. I no longer reacted when I heard the now familiar gunshots from outside the cell. Those shots could be heard several times each day, usually occurring in groups of two to five, beginning at sunrise. The Communists didn't employ what we think of as a firing squad; one pistol shot delivered to the back of the head at close range was sufficient. I wondered how those who had been executed had faced their deaths. It occurred to me that many of those hapless victims were probably no more guilty than I. . . .

Their Ultimate Plan

They came for me one day after I had been in the death cell for about a week, for what I thought would be my last time. Seeing the back door of the cell open very slowly, I looked up to behold the face of the youngest guard that I had ever seen. He spoke to me almost in a whisper. "Come with me." There was a pleasant expression on his face. He escorted me politely down the corridor in the direction of the guard office. Conflicting thoughts rushed through my mind. This is it, I thought. This is exactly the way they would do it: send their youngest and most polite guard to escort me to the place of my execution.

When I entered the guard room, I found another equally young man sitting in a chair behind a desk. He quickly arose, looked at me for a moment as he walked past me, and then asked the first guard to follow him into the hallway. They talked together in whispers for a few seconds before reentering the room. There was an empty expression on their faces—also entirely consistent with what I deemed to be their ultimate plan for me.

Again, there were all kinds of conflicting thoughts going on in my mind, a part of me insisting that these would be my last few minutes alive, another part taking issue with that train of thought entirely. Suddenly, the second guard left the room and disappeared down the hallway. The remaining guard ordered me to sit down in a chair beside a desk. A deathly silence followed, allowing my perplexed mind to work overtime in conflicting speculation. Yes, this is it, I thought. "Well, Larry, are you ready? As ready as I ever will be," I thought. I wondered why they had picked the two youngest men to be participants in all this. Will one of them be required by his officers to pull the trigger and thus prove his loyalty to the system? Yes, they are capable of that, I concluded.

I caught myself searching the inside of the small guard office to see whether I could locate bullet holes in the walls or furniture. There were none that I could see. "They won't kill me in this office," I thought, "but in that special place just outside the latrine," the execution area next to the high wall that the guard had pointed out the first morning of my imprisonment. But even as I had reached this state of mental preparation (or confusion), part of my mind rejected the idea that I was about to die.

The wait for the first guard to return was a long one. At any moment I expected to see him reappear in the doorway accompanied by at least one officer. That never happened. When the guard did return, he was alone. Following a hurried conference in whispers, one of the two guards politely ordered me to stand. The same courteous guard returned me to my cell, leaving me to ponder what might have just taken place. I finally concluded that I had been taken out of my cell for an interrogation that for some reason never came off. It had been a very emotionally draining experience.

I relate this story, in part, to demonstrate that the mind may work against you under stress. The actions and behavior of the two guards, though a little unusual, did not really warrant the conclusion that I had drawn—that I was on my way to my execution. Perhaps once the mind has been thoroughly traumatized, it sometimes misinterprets the information it receives. For whatever reason, the prisoner must be prepared to fight enemies both from within and without.

A Woman Combat Correspondent's Perspective

Marguerite Higgins

Marguerite Higgins was the Far East bureau chief for the New York *Herald Tribune* when the Korean War broke out. She immediately moved to South Korea and reported on the fall of Seoul. The following excerpt is from her bestselling book *War in Korea*. In it she dispels misconceptions about North Korean and Chinese soldiers. She describes a stoic but resourceful enemy who can fight to the death without the benefit of supply lines or luxury. She also reveals a human side to the enemy. Much of Higgins's reporting centers around the role of communism in subverting communities and conscripting unwilling soldiers.

Higgins was the first woman to win a Pulitzer Prize for war correspondence. She died in 1966 after contracting a rare tropical ailment while touring Vietnam, Pakistan, and India.

The Soviet-directed Oriental taught us a great deal about himself in the period between June and December of 1950. He did this through a series of stinging defeats. It is true that in many battles he outnumbered us overwhelmingly. But the enemy's strength is not in numbers alone.

In Korea the oriental peasant, both Chinese and Korean, showed that he could drive a tank, lob a mortar, and fire a machine gun with deadly efficiency. I remember talking to a marine in the Naktong River bulge who said ruefully, "Those gooks can land a mortar right in your hip pocket."

In addition, the enemy can fight on about one fifth of what the United States Army presently considers necessary. The enemy's army has a minimum number of housekeeping and supply services. Beer and mail are not received in front-line foxholes. Trucks carrying goodies from the Post Exchange do not clog the enemy's roads. The proportion of administrative officers to combat officers is low. More soldiers are required to shoot and fewer to do paper work than in the American Army. By our standards, the enemy's medical corps is primitive. But he is accustomed to privation and dirt and has great powers of endurance. The slogan of the Chinese soldier is typical: "First we suffer, then we enjoy."

Communist Officers Possessed Fanatical Devotion

Probably the greatest achievement of the Chinese and North Korean dictatorship is the quality of their officers. Here their system of intensive political indoctrination has certainly paid off. The fanaticism of the officers often kept the North Koreans and Chinese fighting under circumstances in which the enlisted men were eager to surrender.

There was little fundamental difference between the North Korean soldier and the Chinese soldier. This is not surprising, since the nucleus of the North Korean Army was trained in the Chinese Eighth Route Army. If anything, the Chinese were a little smarter, a little better disciplined than the Koreans.

The enemy made maximum use of his great manpower advantage for the infiltration and encirclement of our forces. They combined guerilla tactics with a shrewd use of modern weapons. They used psychological warfare to advantage. They made the most of night attacks, in which assaults were launched to the blowing of bugles, and squads controlled by the shriek of whistles. An amazing number of Chinese and Koreans spoke a little English. These men would strip overcoats and parkas from our dead soldiers and try to make us believe they were friends. Others learned to yell "medic, medic" and trick us into revealing our positions.

Private Carrol Brewer told me of one tactic used by the Chinese in the marine battle out of Yudamni. "They would let us into their foxholes and disappear over a hill. Then at night they would come back by the thousands. And they'd wait until they were practically on top of you before they'd shoot."

They frequently seemed to care very little for life and were willing to die unquestioningly. They would keep right on surging toward a target even though wave after wave of them were blown up in the process.

The Enemy Used Our Equipment Against Us

In their encircling and nipping-off tactics, the Communists often won rich prizes in American equipment. When the enemy broke through our lines on the Kum River, for instance, they scooped up ammunition, artillery guns, machine guns, recoilless weapons, and mortars. The Chinese winter break-through also gave them substantial booty.

This capture of our weapons enabled the enemy to hold out at the beginning in spite of our heavy bombing of North Korean bases. The Communists didn't have to depend on supplies from home bases. They were getting them from us.

The Chinese, and particularly the North Koreans, forage much of what they need in the way of food and services as they go along. They make the local population carry ammunition and cook their food. (It was only very late in the summer that Americans learned to use local citizenry for ammo bearers.) They make use of every conceivable beast of burden, even camels.

The complaint against the Russians made by the German General von Manteuffel [who commanded the Seventh Panzer Division on the eastern front during World War II] could well be repeated against the Reds in Korea. Von Manteuffel said of the Russian Army: "You can't stop them, like an ordinary army, by cutting their communications, because you so rarely find any supply columns to cut."

By comparison with the enemy, the American Army is

road-bound. General Dean of the 24th Division put the problem very neatly when he said, "How am I going to teach these boys that they can't all jeep to battle?"

The Chinese were very short of heavy equipment in the first phases of their intervention. They had to rely mainly on machine guns and grenades, although they did turn American light bazookas against us very effectively. If the numerical odds had been anywhere near even, their lack of heavy equipment could have been a handicap to them. But as it was, their shortage of heavy artillery made it possible for them to hike at night over mountain trails, with the guns and packs on their backs. Then, with the enormous advantage of surprise, they could jump our troops at will.

Blinded by Propaganda

Five years of political indoctrination had put highly effective intellectual blinders on North Korean officers. I was impressed by a talk I had with one North Korean lieutenant. He was among a group of wounded prisoners of war whom I interviewed in our base hospital at Pusan.

"The only reason I am here is because I was unconscious when I was captured," he said. "I would never have surrendered of my own will. I believed with all my heart that I was doing the right thing by fighting for the unification of my country. I believed the people in South Korea were oppressed."

The lieutenant himself was ragged and covered with sores, and he now indicated to the interpreter, an American missionary, that he wanted to say more. It may have been for my benefit, but he added, "Now that I've talked to South Koreans, I believe that all the things we were taught are not true. I feel pity for those who are still fighting, because they do not know the truth."

Apparently this indoctrination is not completely shared, as yet, by the rank and file. Many North Korean enlisted men surrendered. The marines, completely surrounded by the enemy at Hagaru, had a pleasant surprise when two hundred Chinese came voluntarily into camp.

They Suffered Just as We Did

These POWs were reassuring evidence that the enemy was only human. When I was at Koto there were nearly three hundred Chinese POWs in the improvised stockade. I wanted to find out why they seemed to survive the frightful cold better than we did. The answer was that they didn't. Their feet were black with frostbite, and the gangrenous odor of rotting flesh filled the stockade air.

While I was in the stockade a wounded Chinese was brought in on a stretcher. His arms were bent at the elbow, and his hands and feet were frozen marble solid. He was groaning rhythmically.

A wizened Chinese corporal plucked at my sleeve and pointed to his moaning countryman. "That is why we surrender," he said.

These Chinese captured on the northeast front generally wore only tennis shoes and several pairs of socks. Naturally their feet suffered, but the rest of their uniforms—quilted jackets and pants—seemed to keep them sufficiently warm.

The Chinese who surrendered to us in the northeast were the weakest link in the Communist enemy command. Significantly, none ranked higher than corporal. They all said that they had been forced to fight. But this claim may be more representative of innate Chinese diplomacy than the truth. I asked, through my interpreter, Lieutenant Paul Y. Kim, if any of them wanted to go back to China.

All the prisoners gestured "No." The corporal, the oldest of the group and its spokesman, recited reasons that have become decidedly familiar. "We were poor under [Chinese Nationalist president] Chiang [Kai-shek]," he said, "but now we are both poor and cannot do as we want. We cannot move freely from village to village. Many are arrested. We do not wish to fight for the Communists."

These Chinese POWs were ignorant men but they had a very clear idea of their country's relationship to Russia.

"The Russians," said the old corporal, with a distressed sweep of his hands, "are everywhere in China, but especially at the airfields. And it is they who decide."

The original North Korean Army that struck southward on June twenty-fifth probably totaled close to one hundred and fifty thousand men. Even without air power and without sea power, they mauled us badly until the Inchon landing.

An Army of Five Million

Then the Chinese armies stepped in. The Chinese Peoples Liberation Army consists of five million men. But Far Eastern experts say that only two million of these are first-rate front-line troops. These are organized in a system of five field armies.

The Fourth Field Army, the first to intervene in Korea, is led by General Lin Piao. He is forty-two years old and graduated from the Whampoa Military Academy at Canton. He began fighting for the Communists in 1927 and is considered one of Peking's best commanders. The Third Field Army, also in Korea, is led by General Chen Yi, who previously held command of East China.

These forces are not only the best trained but also the best equipped in China. Much of their equipment is American. They seized many American bazookas, jeeps, trucks, and fieldpieces in Manchuria and they captured many American weapons from the Chinese Nationalists [who fled to Formosa, modern-day Taiwan]. They also took over Japanese supplies left behind in Manchuria. The Russians have provided them with tanks. And the Chinese air force, which probably totaled only five hundred planes in January of 1951, may soon be rapidly expanded.

We relearned from the Chinese what we had discovered in fighting the North Koreans. Air power and artillery are not enough when you are vastly outnumbered in mountainous terrain. Even the marines, fully supported by air and equipped with the best American weapons, could not cope with the masses of howling, bugle-blowing Chinese. In the mountains of East Korea ill-equipped Chinese pushed the marines back by sheer weight of numbers. Marine close-support planes, striking sometimes within thirty-five feet of the front lines, saved thousands of lives and won many skir-mishes. But the planes could not win the day.

Compassion for POWs Was by Design

One of the "Eight Rules of Conduct" laid down by Peking provides for the good treatment of captives. It is the Communist theory that this contributes to victory. From time to time the Chinese have made token releases of prisoners, in the hope that the prisoners would report their good treatment and encourage our soldiers to give up. The Chinese were certainly far more correct in their behavior toward captives than were the North Koreans. This is not surprising, as both North and South Koreans are notorious for their cruelty.

I do not believe that the Chinese treatment of prisoners reflects any innate softheartedness. It is a tactic. When barbarism served the purpose better, the Chinese did not hesitate. They certainly caused inhuman suffering by their practice of hurling hand grenades into ambulances, and on one occasion they set fire to a gasoline-soaked truckload of American wounded.

The North Koreans gave the local population the full Communist treatment. Their police-state techniques were far more ruthless than those I had seen in Poland. The Reds seemed in a greater hurry in Korea—perhaps they reasoned that the people had had such a short experience with individual freedom that a return to despotism would not meet with much resistance.

In Seoul the North Koreans jailed key clergymen, including Bishop Patrick J. Byrne. One Catholic priest was murdered and most of the rest were deported to the North. One explanation for this bold persecution is undoubtedly that the Christians are only about a million strong, a decided minority. The Reds must have felt in a position to make an all-out attack against the Church without arousing too much popular indignation.

The Reds were also astute at using food as a political weapon. They took over all stocks of rice. Then families whose children joined the Communist League [an organization dedicated to spreading communism] got special ration cards. The same was true of workers who enrolled in Communist unions.

The invaders carried on a systematic terror campaign against all people who had ever been associated with Americans. Many thousand alleged "pro-Americans" were thrown into prison and all their property was confiscated. The Seoul newspapers were labeled pro-American and their plants annexed by the Reds.

Their formula for taking over the government of the important cities was the same everywhere. A municipal administration, complete with mayor and cabinet, was formed in Pyongyang and sent to the city immediately after capture. All key posts were filled by trusted emissaries from the North. Sometimes local elections were held, carefully designed to make the conquered areas an integral part of the northern government.

In some places the Reds issued decrees dispossessing landowners who held more than a certain prescribed acreage. In the short period of the first occupation they were unable to do a thorough job of this. Their decrees aroused little enthusiasm because they were coupled with very high crop-delivery requirements.

Even North Koreans Feared the Communists

One way the Communists really made themselves unpopular was by introducing forced conscription of young men into the North Korean Army. They would go into houses and farm dwellings at night and, often at pistol point, force young Koreans to march off of training centers.

At Hagaru we had an example of local hostility toward the invading Chinese armies. Colonel Bankson Holcomb, 1st Marine Division intelligence officer, told me that some of the townspeople had actually come to him and asked him to burn their homes so that the Chinese could not get them. Of course he didn't do it, but it was an interesting insight into the depth of their feeling.

The pitiful swarms of refugees who fled South in the wake of our retreating army were irrefutable evidence of how much the people feared the Reds. They waded across icy streams and crawled painfully across broken ridges rather than stay at home and face the Communists. At the Hungan beachhead Rear Admiral Doyle radioed to Tokyo, "My personal observation is that if the lift were available we could denude North Korea of its civilian population. Almost all of them want to go to South Korea."

In my first visit to Seoul in May of 1950 there were a number of Korean newspapermen who believed some of the Communist propaganda. They felt that unity was better than two antagonistic Koreas, even if it meant Communist domination. I tried to revisit some of these men when the second Red siege of Seoul was threatening. But their taste of Red rule between June and September had been enough. They had been among the first to go south, and I could not find them.

It is true, of course, that in the early days of the Chinese Communist struggle the agrarian reforms won much popular support in China. Probably the Chinese must have been comparatively gentle in their demands for compulsory crop deliveries. They were seeking to win over the Chinese people by persuasion. But the Reds in Korea were backed from the start by the Soviet. They had absolute power and did not need to persuade. In any event, the Korean farmers with whom I talked near Wonsan and in the Hungnam Hamhung Plain expressed great bitterness against the government. They claimed that taxes and quotas were so high that there was nothing left for their own families. After our December retreat from the North thousands of farmers abandoned their own land to become propertyless refugees in South Korea.

It is high time to evaluate what these months in Korea have taught us. Korea has proved decisively to the world that the oriental peasant is an efficient fighting man and that the new militarism of China has produced a first-class army.

Until now the democratic world has relied on technological supremacy and the possession of superior firearms to win its battles with the oriental world. Now the oriental world has most of these weapons, in addition to man power. The Chinese are a powerful instrument of the Soviet, which has boldly attacked the United States and the United Nations.

By challenging us with force, the enemy has confronted the free world with a series of choices, all of them unpleasant.

A U.S. Soldier's Perspective

Bob Roy

Before the invasion of South Korea, the North Korean and Chinese armies were thought to be disorganized, ill equipped, and lacking training. U.S. forces quickly discovered that intelligence to be inaccurate. Bob Roy, an army private based in Japan, was sent with a hastily assembled battalion to delay the North Korean invasion until reinforcements could be assembled. The unit was called Task Force Smith, named after Lieutenant Colonel Brad Smith, who would command the unit. The following excerpt is Roy's personal account of the rout of Task Force Smith, which illustrates how ill-prepared the United States was in the Korean War.

When we heard the news of the invasion we didn't pay any attention to it. The officers did, but we didn't.

On the last day of June we got paid, and as usual the whole camp cleared out except for the guys who had duty. Everybody else went into town and stayed until the midnight curfew. At midnight we all came in to the barracks pretty well feeling our oats. We'd just gotten to bed when one of our lieutenants came in, threw on the lights and said, "Pack your gear. We're headed for Korea."

That's when we knew the war was on.

I was on a 75mm recoilless rifle. Nine months before I'd been in the Military Police. M Company was originally an MP unit. Then one day they came around and said, "All right, you're all in the infantry."

Bob Roy, "First Blood," *No Bugles, No Drums: An Oral History of the Korean War,* by Rudi Tomedi. New York: John Wiley & Sons, 1993. Copyright © 1993 by Rudi Tomedi. Reproduced by permission of the publisher.

How did I get on a 75? "There you are. This is what you're going to do. You're the volunteer."

The 75 is basically a big bazooka mounted on a tripod. Each gun has a five-man crew. It's an awkward weapon, because it gives your position away. It has a big backflash, and it also blows up a big cloud of dust. It's like saying, "Here we are."

There was supposed to be four 75s going over, but two got delayed. Two went through. I happened to be one of the lucky ones that went through.

From Camp Wood we rode up to the airfield at Itazuke in trucks. I remember the Japanese guard waving us out the gate. We'd left all our personal stuff in the barracks. We all thought we'd be back in a week or so.

I think the ride took three or four hours. I remember it was raining. When we got to the airfield we stood in formation in the rain with the two rifle companies. Brad Smith [the lieutenant colonel in command of Task Force Smith, the first unit sent to Korea] was there, talking to General Dean, the 24th Division commander. I guess Smith was getting his instructions. Then Smith saluted, and we were ordered into the planes.

I believe they were C-54s [cargo transport planes]. Six of them. Our gun was already in the plane, all strapped down with the ammunition. On the flight over I thought we were going to hit the water. We flew at wave-top level to stay out of the radar. Add that to the fact that that was my first-ever plane flight, and you got one nervous kid sitting in that canvas seat.

A lot of the guys were writing letters, hoping to get them out somehow, because the families weren't notified. Nobody knew we were going. And of course nobody knew what the hell was going to happen when we got there.

We landed near Pusan [a port city in southeastern Korea] on the first of July, and it took us four days to get into position. First we were put on a train and went as far as Taejon [a city in western South Korea]. At Taejon we loaded onto trucks, and from there we moved a little farther north each day. I had no idea where we were going. All I knew was we were headed for the front, wherever the hell that was. I was only a PFC [private first class] and when they tell you to go somewhere, you go. You don't ask questions.

What I remember most about those four days was not getting any sleep. And the flies. The flies would carry you away. We were in this little Korean village, before we went up to our final position, and [war correspondent] Marguerite Higgins showed up and started interviewing us, and the flies . . . we were spitting them out of our mouths as we talked.

And the stench. The Koreans put human excrement in their rice paddies, and God did it smell.

Moving into Position

We got to our final positions on July fifth, at two in the morning. The infantry started digging in. My 75 they put on one of the highest knolls. We got off our truck and went straight up the hill. The lieutenant told us where he wanted the gun, and up we went.

I learned later that while we were still moving north Brad Smith had gone up ahead and personally picked the position we were going to fight from. It was a good position. We were set up along a ridge that ran at right angles to the main highway that came south from Seoul. The infantry was dug in to the left and right of the road. My 75 covered the road, and the other gun was placed over near a railroad. From up where we were, when daylight came, we could see two or three miles ahead of us.

About seven in the morning I decided to open a can of C rations ["canned" army field rations], and that's when we saw the tanks. I just dropped the can. What the hell was this? Nobody told us about any tanks.

Before I fired the first round I counted thirty-five tanks coming down the road. Everybody was shitting their pants. From what I understand now, the South Koreans had been running from the tanks, and they wanted somebody up there who wasn't going to run. But at the time we weren't told that. We weren't told anything. We were all eighteen, nineteen years old, a bunch of cocky guys. We didn't know what to expect, and we didn't think too much about it. I think if I'd been thirty years old I would've turned around and run.

We didn't realize what we'd gotten into until we saw those tanks. But by then we were in it.

We had no armor-piercing shells, so we tried to stop them by hitting the tracks. We would've been better off throwing Molotov cocktails [homemade fire bombs] at them. Some rounds were duds, some were even smoke rounds. We could see them bounce right off the tanks.

We fired as fast as we could. As soon as we'd get a round into the breech we'd cover our ears and let it go, get another one in, fire that one . . . but they went right through us, right on down the road.

A round from one of the tanks hit right in front of my gun. I saw it coming. I saw the turret turn. We worked as fast as we could to try and get off another round, but the tank shot first, and all five of us were thrown back over the hill from the concussion and the earth hitting us in the face. Our ears were ringing. We were all disoriented, couldn't function at all for five or ten minutes.

But the gun was all right. The lieutenant, he wanted us to go back and get it. The tank was still there, with its turret pointed right at us. I said to him, "I'm not going up there until that tank moves." I disobeyed a direct order. I said, "If you want that gun, you go get it."

He didn't go. The gun just sat there, and the tank waited there for a while, and we kept peeking over the hill, watching the tank, until it moved farther down the road.

We stayed there for a while longer and just watched the tanks. A few had stopped alongside the road and were firing into our positions, into the infantry, but none of them stayed around for long. Then our officers moved us across the road and behind a hill where the mortars were.

The Last Smoke
By this time, eight, nine in the morning, it was raining like hell. The mortars were right behind us, firing for all they

were worth. The North Korean infantry had come down the road in trucks, and had gotten out of the trucks and started moving around our flanks. I didn't actually see the North Koreans deploy, because our view was blocked by the hill in front of us, but we knew their infantry must have come up behind the tanks because the mortars and our own infantry were all firing like crazy.

Me, I couldn't see anything to shoot at. So we got under a poncho, me and another guy, and we sat there smoking a cigarette.

An officer came by and yelled down at us, "What the hell are you doing?"

"We're having a smoke."

He says, "You're about to die."

"Yeah," we said, "we're havin' our last smoke."

That's the way it was for us. That was our state of mind. We'd been told how the North Koreans were a ragtag army, couldn't fight worth a shit, couldn't shoot straight, all that baloney. And what did we know? A bunch of kids? We just believed what we were told. And it was raining like hell. And our ammo's no good. We had nothing at all to fight with.

We'd been in trouble from the beginning, only now we knew it.

Hell, it was even worse than we knew. By now all the radios were out. The tanks had run over the communications wire, and the ones in the jeeps got wet from the rain and just stopped working. The infantry was strung out along the ridge, and we were just behind them, and there was no communication between any of the units.

I heard Brad Smith give the order to withdraw. He was up on the hill behind us. He stood up there and gave the order verbally. Just yelled it out. I don't remember exactly what he said, if he said "Every man for himself," but they were words to that effect.

So we got the word, but I found out later that one platoon never did get the word to pull out. They were left there all by themselves. Some of those guys eventually got out, and some didn't.

Scattering in All Directions

As soon as we heard the withdrawal order we took off down the hill and crossed the road, but by now the North Koreans had gotten behind us. They had the high ground, and I was down in a rice paddy and all friggin' hell broke loose. It sounded like a bunch of bees. Friggin' bullets bouncing all over the place.

Everybody just kept going, as fast as they could. Slipping and sliding through the rice paddies. Like I say, I don't remember the exact words Brad Smith used, but by now it was definitely every man for himself. Nobody wanted to be the last one out of there.

We were supposed to destroy our gun, but we didn't have anything to destroy it with. There's a self-destruct charge you drop in the breech. We didn't have any of those. We didn't have any grenades. As gunners we didn't even have rifles. All we had was our .45s [automatic pistols].

We just left the gun where it was.

Normally what you do when you have to withdraw is you set up a rendezvous point. Then you retreat in an orderly fashion toward that point. But there was never any rendezvous point. Nobody told us anything. So we all took off on our own.

I was with a squad of guys who all got captured. Every one of them except me. I went over a railroad embankment, running like a bastard, because the North Koreans were still firing at us from the hills. Everybody was with me when I went over the embankment, but after running three or four hundred yards I turned around and, Jesus, I'm all alone.

I'm in the middle of all these rice paddies, and I'm thinking, Where the hell is everybody?

I found out, forty years later, that everybody else went down the *right* side of the railroad tracks. They went due south, where the North Korean tanks were, and they got captured. Most of them spent the war as POWs. I went down the left side, kind of southeast, because I wasn't about to go where those tanks were.

I ran into some guys from one of the infantry companies.

They told me what happened up on the ridge. They'd made a pretty good fight of it, but then their ammunition ran out. They were going southeast too, and I joined up with them, and we just kept walking. It was still raining. Just pouring down. We didn't know where we were going. We finally ran into some people from the 34th Regiment, which was deployed south of us, but we had no idea they were there. We were just trying to get away from the North Koreans.

Those people in the 34th had just gotten orders to pull back. They had a sergeant with them who was wounded, and I was O type and I volunteered to give him a pint of blood. I did that because they said they'd give me a ride. Well, I gave him a pint of my blood, and they all loaded up on a jeep, and guess what? There was no room for a ride. I had to walk. It wasn't funny, because I had to walk almost forty miles before we finally stopped and got reorganized. What was left of us.

We were on the Kum River waiting to be relieved by the 19th Infantry when General [Walton] Walker [commander of the Eighth Army] showed up. He stood next to his jeep and gave us a talk. "If they come across this river," he says, "you guys are to stay here and fight to the death." Then he jumps in his jeep and takes off.

And we're all saying, "Yeah, sure."

They got tanks, and we got nothing to knock them out with. I still had only a .45 at the time, and I think six rounds of ammunition.

You've got to understand what it feels like to be in combat and not have enough ammunition, or have a weapon that don't work. The feeling of helplessness. What I'm saying is, it's easy to sit back and say, Well, those guys ran. Sure we ran. But what did we have to fight with?

You read about a lot of the wounded and litter cases being left behind. But I saw guys who should've gotten medals. I saw guys carrying other guys who had been shot in the legs. There were a lot of guys trying to help other people out. I saw a buddy of mine stay behind to lay down covering fire, and I don't know to this day if he got out of there. Everybody was trying to help out the best they could.

I lost a lot of friends there. One of them was my best buddy, John Holland. We used to call him Baby Face. He was only seventeen. A seventeen-year-old kid from Ohio. He was my gun loader and my bunkmate. In Japan we used to go out to the cabarets and have a few beers together. He was taken prisoner by the North Koreans and died in captivity.

We were sent over there to delay the North Koreans. We delayed them seven hours. Don't ask me if it was worth it. We were a bunch of kids and we were just trying to do our jobs.

Americans Are Corrupt

Tai Ching-Shan

During the Korean War, U.S./UN prisoners of war (POWs) were severely mistreated by their North Korean captors. Many died from malnutrition, abuse, and exposure, especially during the harsh winters. The POWs were also subjected to daily reeducation lectures about communism and were coerced to renounce the actions of their countries. When the Chinese entered the war on the side of the North Koreans, they assumed control of the POW camps. The Chinese recognized the bargaining value of having living prisoners and slowly improved the conditions of the camps.

The following is a propagandist account of the Korean War as told by Tai Ching-Shan, a soldier in the Chinese Volunteer Army (CVA). Ching-Shan's account exaggerates U.S. "capitalist corruption" and extols the virtues of the CVA, including its clement treatment of prisoners.

The sound of firing gradually faded into the distance as our front lines pushed south. Late that night I went through a snowstorm with an escort team to a height east of Kunu-ni to take over a batch of captives who had just been sent back from the front. They were being temporarily kept in an air-raid shelter in the mountainside.

As we approached the entrance, two guards came up and told us laughingly, "This is an exhibition hall of invading armies. We've got not only Syngman Rhee [president of the Republic of Korea] puppets, but Americans, Englishmen, Canadians and Turks. It's really a complete assortment!"

"Yes, indeed," another soldier grinned. "Yesterday [U.S. general Douglas] MacArthur ordered them to drive across

Tai Ching-Shan, *A Volunteer Soldier's Day: Recollections by Men of the Chinese People's Volunteers in the War to Resist U.S. Aggression and Aid Korea*. Peking: Foreign Language Press, 1961. Copyright © 1956 by the People's Literature Publishing House. Reproduced by permission of the publisher.

the Yalu River [which runs between North Korea and China], but they've come to spend Christmas here instead. How disobedient of them! What a pity we don't have Christmas on our calendar."

We all laughed.

Still smiling, I entered the cave with Lao Ho, our English interpreter. Several hundred metres long, it was jammed with seated prisoners. There was barely room to walk. After pushing out a little space for ourselves, we turned on all our flashlights and began recording the names and nationalities of the captives.

While we were registering the Americans, Englishmen and Canadians, one prisoner only stared, speechless, and shook his head. Another prisoner beside the wall stood up and said:

"He's a Turk. He doesn't understand English." And he added with a proud smile, "I am an interpreter of the Turkish Brigade. If you gentlemen wish, I can translate for you."

Lao Ho looked at me and laughed. "[President Harry] Truman is certainly thoughtful. He even sends us a Turkish translator."

After a half hour, the air in the cave was becoming rather stuffy. We let the prisoners go out for walks, in groups.

The second group contained an American major. As he emerged from the cave he said to Lao Ho, "You ought to let the whites out first. That's the usual rule."

"We treat all prisoners alike, regardless of their nationality or colour," Lao Ho replied evenly.

"But in the United States, white men always get preference," the tactless major argued. "Negroes are born inferior. Their blood . . ."

"Shut your mouth!" snapped Lao Ho. "This isn't the United States. You'll kindly refrain from slandering the Negro people. It's only under a regime of Wall Street buccaneers that racial discrimination is preached as a cultural and moral virtue!"

The stupid major, apparently realizing his new status at last, silently hung his head and walked away.

Eager to Return to the Front Lines

Treading carefully on the hard-packed slippery snow, we escorted the prisoners towards the rear. They made a long snaking line on the highway; from where I was, neither its head nor its tail could be seen. One of our guards was spaced between every ten prisoners. Because I understood a little English I was put in charge of twelve enemy officers.

No sooner was the order to rest passed down the line than the captives immediately stretched out indolently on the ground. Hands clasped behind my back, I gazed off at distant artillery flashes in the night sky. How I wished we could deliver the prisoners quickly, so that I could catch up with our forces fighting their way south.

As I stood lost in thought, something hard and cold was thrust into my hand. I pulled away in surprise, and a shiny wrist-watch dropped to the snowy road. A U.S. captain standing beside me grinned ingratiatingly.

"What are you up to?" I demanded sternly.

"There are no other Chinese around." He picked up the watch and slyly proffered it to me.

I couldn't control my revulsion. Pointing my finger at him I said, "Listen to what I'm saying—I don't want your dirty bribe!"

He stared at me uncomprehendingly. "That's the sixth one who wouldn't take my watch," he muttered. "They're a strange crowd!"

"The seventh won't take it either," I told him. "Your American way of life doesn't work here."

"War gives men a chance to get rich," he assured me solemnly. "We all made money in Germany during World War II."

"We're not Hitler's Nazi army," I reminded him. "And we're not one of your money-mad armies from a capitalist country either. We are the Chinese People's Volunteers. Never forget that."

He slumped to the ground like a deflated balloon. Holding his precious watch, he gazed at it thoughtfully.

We Sacrificed Our Own Comfort

Shortly before dawn, we assembled all the prisoners on a river bank.

Peering through the night mists, I could see the river—a hundred and more metres wide—swirling rapidly between the mountains flanking it on both sides. I could clearly hear the thud of blocks of ice colliding in midstream. There was a temporary bridge, but it was very narrow. Only one man could cross at a time.

Just then, a large body of our forces began agilely crossing the bridge, heading south. Waiting troops stretched in a long line. I thought to myself: We've got quite a big batch of prisoners who have to be sent north. If we use the bridge we'll hold up the troop movement. But if we wait, it will be daylight before we can deliver the prisoners to their destination. . . . I was growing very anxious when our escort commander called:

"We'll ford the river. Let our people go across first, then the prisoners."

As we took off our clothes and walked down to the river's edge, the prisoners stood on the bank and looked fearfully at the flowing chunks of ice. Persuasion, urging—nothing could induce them to move. The sight of the frigid water chilled their invaders' swagger.

What could we do? Finally, we talked the matter over with the commander of one of the waiting battalions. He agreed to order three of his companies to ford the river together with our escort guards, and let the prisoners use the bridge in their place.

The northwest wind howled through the river gorge. Step by step we waded forward. The frigid December water ate into our bones. Our teeth chattered; floating slabs of ice stabbed us like knives. In the middle, the river grew deeper. Waves threatened to knock us off our feet. Retaining our balance only with the greatest effort, we pushed on and reached the opposite shore.

We dressed and ran up and down the bank to get warm. The prisoners came slowly across the bridge. They looked at us with surprise and respect. The U.S. captain who had tried to bribe me held up his thumb in a gesture of admiration.

"Your treatment of prisoners is certainly the humanest in the world," he cried. "God will bless you!"

"And God may even let a little light creep into that dirty soul of yours!" I thought contemptuously.

Explaining the War: The Government's Perspective

Dean Acheson

On January 16, 1951, John Moullette, a young marine corporal, wrote a letter to his father questioning the direction of U.S. foreign policy. Moullette had just finished a tour of duty in World War II and was getting ready to go to college. But to his dismay his reserve unit was reactivated to fight in Korea. Moullette's father, Clarence, an assistant to the mayor of Camden, New Jersey, forwarded the letter to Secretary of State Dean Acheson asking him to help answer some tough questions. Acheson replied with a long letter that detailed the ideals behind President Truman's policies. The letters were later released to the press and published by the *New York Times* as well as other papers across the country.

Acheson was one of the architects of post–World War II American foreign policy. Acheson advocated a strong role for the United States in controlling the spread of communism. He oversaw the implementation of the Truman Doctrine, which held that America should intervene militarily when a country is in danger of falling to Communist insurgency, and he helped create the Marshall Plan, which provided financial aid for weakened European nations that were in danger of falling to communism following World War II.

January 19th, 1951

Letter from Mr. Moullette to Secretary Acheson. Enclosed, is a letter I received from my son this morning on my arrival at my office. I am sending it to you, since it is a letter which

Dean Acheson, "The Answer to Youth's Bewilderment," *Department of the State Bulletin*, March 19, 1951.

reflects the loose thinking on the part of many of our legislators and publishers—it is a letter filled with answerable questions, but questions which require much in knowledge, substantial qualifications which can and should be made understandable—since the American people as a whole are a provincial lot.

This lad of mine is 24 years old, a Corporal in the Marine Corps at Camp Pendleton, California. He served with the 1st Division from 1944 to August 1946. Last September, he was hoping to enter Cornell University to take his course in Hotel Management. Instead, he went back in the Marine Corps, a Reserve. He was then, and I suspect now, bitter about it all. It so happens, that in September 1949 I warned him not to put too much stock in his future, since I was positive we would be involved somewhere in the world before another year was out. He, my wife and many of my friends made life miserable for me, since they said I was warmongering, when I was only evaluating the news as it was brought to me by a world press.

This lad has been raised in the traditions which have been prevalent in this country since Colonial days—his schooling is that of the average public school pupil, and he has had the advantage of books, magazines, newspapers from all over the world—he has traveled widely for his age, working on tramp steamers and tankers, and the United States is as his back yard at home, he knows it from personal visits.

He Needs to Understand

The tenor of his letter about "foreign policy" leaves me cold and my reply to him will be an explanation that foreign policy is always fluid, that it must be so and has been so since 1914 because of certain inescapable facts. I will explain that we are a gullible people, that we won (or helped win) two wars and lost both times the peace, because we regarded winning wars in the same manner we regard winning a football match. I will tell him something of the different mores of various people, of their hatreds, their jealousies.

I will tell him that the broad policies of our foreign policy is laid down in the Constitution of the United States, in the convictions of our people and their attitudes toward all peoples, all over the world.

I will send him a copy of an address of mine, which he said was too deep for him to understand when he read it in its formative stage. I will try to open his eyes to an understanding of the forces about him which are inimicable to the general good of our people—to the powers which can be wielded to destroy a man, no matter how sincere and true he has been. . . . I will indicate to him that the American people in their utter provincialism are tremendously jealous of their rights and prerogatives as free born Americans, that they want the fruits thereof, but detest its responsibilities—that there are many men to advance their own interests against the interests of the whole people, take advantage of the situations brought about by the general misunderstanding which have been fostered by a press which is venal.

What I am going to tell him of foreign policy will be my experiences in most of the countries of the world, where I have seen my own countrymen reflect the worst of their natures, since they were of the opinion that they were a race apart. I will tell him something of the spread of the Common Law throughout the world by the British, whom he had been taught by a venal press to despise, and it has been hard to offset his distrust of the British even though he has close blood relatives in England, and more of them in Denmark and France.

Mr. Secretary, I have written you a long letter about a letter, but, what actually was also a motivation was a telephone call I received this morning from one of the principals of one of our High Schools. He related to me that his teachers absolutely refused to take Civil Defense seriously, that it was a tempest in a tea pot and, anyhow it was the figment of the administration's imagination that caused all the furore—that we would never be bombed or otherwise attacked, note the remarks of various Senators and Congressmen, and anyway, what was it you read in the press.

I have had members of my own party discount the sincere efforts of the President of the United States, simply because they wished in that way to resist the necessity of facing up to a world that is becoming increasingly more atavistic and reprehensible.

They Want What We Have

Mr. Secretary, I have lived on every continent, worked in most of the countries of the world, or visited them and I have a working knowledge of ten languages, none of them taught to me academically but which I have learned because I needed them. I see about me so many things which are left undone, which should be done, and I want more than anything else to wake my countrymen up to the necessity of realizing we are not living in a chocolate coated world, but one that is armed to the teeth against us by and through actual armor or armed against us in propagating the belief that we have only a nickel under foot to motivate our activities.

I know of personal knowledge that most of the peoples of the world have a sneaking respect for us, that they like us fairly well for ourselves alone, that they fear us far more than we fear them, but all of whom could be turned against us simply because they are jealous of our way of life which we have earned for ourselves by hard work and ingenuity. I hope you will help me with this letter to my son.

16 January, 1951—Tuesday
Letter from Johnnie Moullette to His Father. I just finished reading from the Los Angeles *Examiner* the impeachment resolution against Dean Acheson which was introduced into the California State Senate by State Senator Jack B. Tenney, Republican, from Los Angeles. [Acheson was accused by Republicans of being a Communist sympathizer. A resolution was passed to fire Acheson, but Truman ripped the resolution into pieces.] I can't help but think that the American people, Democrat and Republican alike, are "fed

up" with the Administration and its foreign policy.

The way Truman is appropriating money is outrageous. It is my belief that he is taking anyone's word for it and spending money uselessly and needlessly. At present he is asking Congress for 71.5 billion dollars which would cost each American $468.00.

Don't you think that our "foreign policy" is fouled up a bit? What right have we to refuse Red China entree into the United Nations? I think she (Red China) has a right to voice her opinions about what is to take place in the Far East. After all, isn't she a country out there just as Venezuela or Brazil is in our hemisphere? I say, "Let Red China into the U.N. and let her voice her vote and her opinions on what is to take place in the Far East."

A Needless Waste

The needless waste of life in Korea, on both sides, is shameful to the human race. Fighting won't settle anything. The only thing that I can see is being proven in Korea is: "Might over what *may* be right," Red China being the "might." The problem of Red China vs. the world, or the best part of it, has to be settled at the round table and eventually it will be. Red China will be admitted to the U.N. So the U.N. will have lost the first round. . . .

I thought that only Congress could declare war. Why doesn't Congress either declare war against Red China or stop Truman from sending American troops throughout the world? Why should we take the brunt of it all? If the other countries in the U.N. won't supply the needed men and money then we should pull out of Korea and if need be, out of the U.N. . . .

The morale of the fighting man is very low. Mainly because the American people aren't behind him. Here at Pendleton most of these men know what war is or what its after-effects are and will be. Just last night at the "slop-shute" (beer-hall) the men, not one or two, but the majority, were complaining about the way we were tricked into this. Everyone seems to have nothing but disfavorable thoughts, and remarks about the foreign policy. These men aren't afraid to fight, it's just that they have no cause to fight. If ordered to, we will but only because of the obligation we have to each other. I guess it's a form of "Brotherly Love."

Our only hope is that men our age throughout the world feel the same way and will state so to their leaders. By rebellion or other ways. After the loss of life, and property from the last war, everyone should want only peace. I believe that the people of our level want only peace but that the leaders (including Truman) are afraid to admit they are wrong and are ashamed to admit it for fear they will lose face. It looks that way, Dad!

I guess I've tired your eyes by now so I'll secure for now. Good luck in your defense job.

Love,

JOHNNIE

P.S. I may be a rebel but these are my own thoughts and convictions. . . .

February 23, 1951

Letter from Secretary Acheson to Mr. Moullette. I have thought a great deal about the letter from your son, which you sent me, and your problem in answering it wisely and helpfully. It brought back many memories to me of ten years ago when my own son was in college, before he went to the Pacific, and I used to sit with him and his friends and talk over their problems which loomed ahead of them—and all of us.

I thought then—and think now—that the real problem lies deeper than the questioning of particular decisions—even the important ones which distress your son. It lies in the fact—for which we may thank God—that these boys have been brought up in the fundamental decency and rightness of American life. They have lived in communities where they have breathed in with the air truth and tolerance of others' interests, generosity and good nature, hard work, honesty and fairness. To all of them opened the opportunity for happy and constructive lives, their own homes and families, work to do, a part to play in the community in a hundred ways. They saw no problems, here at home, that would not yield to effort, ingenuity, and the give-and-take of people who believed in the same right values.

Now, just at the moment when they were about to enter fully as grown men in this world, its promise is dashed. In its place, they find hardship, loneliness, uncertainty, danger. They are separated from family and friends. Even worse, they are denied the natural development of their lives. The fact that this happens to them because some distant and shadowy figures in the [Soviet] Kremlin, controlling millions of people far from them, are setting out to make impossible such lives as they had every right and hope to have, does not help their frustration and bitterness.

This agony of spirit, so understandable and right, makes it hard to believe that so monstrous an evil can exist in a world based upon infinite mercy and justice.

But the fact is that it does exist. The fact is that it twists and tortures all our lives. And, I believe, to each of us in this case as in so many others, the great thing is not what happens to us but how we bear what happens to us.

For our country, and for most of us as individuals, the period which has passed since V-E [Victory in Europe] and V-J [Victory in Japan] Days has been one of cruel disappointment, slowly forming resolution, and, finally, great determination and effort. The high hopes, for which great sacrifices were made during the War, did not come to ready fruition. That did not mean that these hopes—for peace, and for a good life for all—were wrong, or that the principles of freedom and justice on which they were based were not worthy of these sacrifices.

What it did mean was that it was going to be a good deal harder to build the kind of world we wanted, than we thought it was going to be.

We started out, even before the War had ended, building the foundation of the structure of peace, of law and order in the world, in the United Nations. We hoped that all nations would work together in bringing this about.

Our Way of Life Is Being Challenged

We came very close to realizing this aspiration. An international organization has been started functioning, and in some cases, it has performed extremely successfully. The role of the United Nations in the disputes in Palestine and in Indonesia suggest that, far from being discouraged, we should be heartened by the progress that has been made.

However as it became clear that the rulers of the Soviet Union not only were not interested in cooperating with us, but were challenging the survival of our free institutions, and the independence of all nations, we have been obliged to build up our strength again, all of us.

In some ways, this is an ancient problem. Our forebears on this continent had it cruelly impressed upon them that the liberty we enjoy is not won and preserved without unremitting effort, without sacrifice, without "eternal vigilance." But we had for so long enjoyed the blessings of freedom, that we had come to accept this condition as automatically assured. It has fallen to us—to your son's generation, and to ours—to take up again the defense of freedom against the challenge of tyranny.

In other ways, this is a new problem. Our country, which has risen to a position of unprecedented power and eminence in the world, is seeking to use that power in such a way as to help bring about a peaceful international order. This means that we have to be doing two things at once: while we move ahead in our efforts to build the kind of a world in which we can all live together peacefully and in common helpfulness, we are at the same time protecting ourselves from being overrun by the tyranny which is run from Moscow. I have sometimes compared this two-pronged effort as being like the way our ancestors had to have some men drilling and keeping watch from the blockhouses, while others went on, tilling the fields.

In a sense, we are standing with one foot in the world of our hopes for a future order among nations, and the other foot in the world of power. Both of these are part of the present reality. Unless we are strong enough—we and the other free nations—to prevent the Soviet rulers from extending their control over the entire world, then we shall never have the chance to help build the kind of a world we all want.

Freedom Does Not Come Easily

There are many terrible heartbreaks in this course of action, but there is no easier way to a peaceful world. Your son asks in his letter whether Korea proves anything. That he is heartsick over the loss of life and the destruction in Korea is right and good, and reflects what must be the instinctively humane feelings of good men everywhere. But I hope he will come to see that Korea proves—has already proved—a great deal. In Korea, the men and the nations who love freedom and who believe in the United Nations have made it clear that they are willing to fight for these things. By standing firm against aggression in Korea, we are doing our best to prevent the world from following the road which led us, twice in recent times, to World War. The heroic sacrifices which are now being made in Korea may enable the world to pass through this time of hostility and tension without the catastrophe, the greater destruction and the immeasurably greater sacrifices of a world conflict.

I know that these thoughts I have written to you will not answer all the questions which you have touched on in your thoughtful letter, or which your son has mentioned. These are hard and complicated problems, for which there are no easy answers, and which a short letter could not deal with adequately. What I am concerned about is not that your son should feel that I, or the Administration, or the Government is right on any particular issue. It is good that he should question whether the steps we are taking are right or are wrong. But what is important is that he feel, and that all our young people feel, a strong faith in the validity and the reality of the ideals on which this country was founded and on which it now endeavors to guide its actions. So long as our young people are steadfast in this faith, we can be assured of the vitality of our society, and its ability to go on meeting the challenges of the future.

4

NEGOTIATING PEACE OR GIVING UP

The Communists Prevented a Negotiated Peace

C. Turner Joy

After a year of bloody stalemate, the United States, South Korea, and North Korea began to discuss an armistice. Vice Admiral C. Turner Joy was chosen as chief UN delegate to conduct negotiations, which were held at Kaesong, the old Korean capital. Joy writes that the accords began slowly since neither side trusted the other. Ideological and cultural differences, as well as the obstinacy of Communist leaders, made achieving even the simplest goals difficult. All of these factors, including limitations placed on Joy by the UN, contributed to delaying the peace process for years. Frustrated by the lack of progress, Joy asked to be reassigned. He was tendered the position of superintendent of the U.S. Naval Academy, but he was diagnosed with leukemia a month later. Joy died in June 1956 after a distinguished career. The following excerpt is taken from his diary of experiences at the armistice conference, where officials from the countries involved in the Korean War sought to end the dispute.

On May 22, 1952, . . . when I turned over my job as senior delegate of the UNC [United Nations Command] Delegation to Major General Harrison, the wording of only one paragraph, in an armistice document containing sixty-two paragraphs, stood in the way of an honorable agreement. That controversial paragraph, as you know, deals with the much publicized prisoner of war issue. After a bitter verbal

C. Turner Joy, *Negotiating While Fighting: The Diary of Admiral C. Turner Joy at the Korean Armistice Conference*, edited by Allan E. Goodman. Stanford, CA: Hoover Institution Press, 1978. Copyright © 1978 by the Board of Trustees of the Leland Stanford Junior University. Reproduced by permission.

battle lasting over ten months all paragraphs but that one had been agreed upon.

The story of our battle in reaching agreement on the sixty-one paragraphs is much too long and involved to tell you tonight. But the story of *why* our battle was so long and bitter and *why* we could not reach agreement on the prisoner of war question is much more quickly and easily told. I shall confine my remarks primarily to the latter story in the hope that it will give you an insight into the difficulties of trying to negotiate with the Communists.

Beginning the Peace Talks

Now if you remember, when Jacob Malik, Soviet representative in the United Nations, made his proposal for a Korean truce on June 23, 1951, many people believed the Communists wanted an Armistice badly enough to agree on reasonable terms. I was one of them. Their armies had taken a beating on the battlefield the month before when they had attacked in strength. In that abortive May offensive they had suffered some 200,000 casualties. The Eighth Army had counterattacked and was slowly pushing them beyond the 38th parallel. Though by no means decisively defeated, the Communists were in a bad way and needed a cease-fire to repair their battered war machine.

Consequently, since we were negotiating from a position of military strength, it did not surprise me too much when we of the UNC Delegation made progress in those earlier days of the Armistice Conference. To be sure it was slower progress than anyone had expected, due mainly to irritating interruptions and Communist intransigence, but it was progress nonetheless. For example, it took only ten meetings to reach agreement on an agenda for the Conference in spite of a wide difference of opinion as to the wording and contents of the agenda.

The first of these agenda items reads as follows: "The fixing of a military demarcation line between both sides so as to establish a demilitarized zone as a basic condition for the cessation of hostilities in Korea."

On July 26 when the two delegations began the main discussions on this item the Communists were adamant in their insistence that the demarcation line separating the two forces must be none other than the 38th parallel. Our own position was that the demarcation line should be based generally on the battle line, which, as you will remember, was considerably north of the 38th parallel in all areas of military significance. We were not of a mind to save Communist face by withdrawing from hard-won ground above the 38th parallel thus erasing any penalty for their war of aggression. The Communists presented many arguments in support of the 38th parallel, none of which were any good and all of which were refuted many times. Some were downright ridiculous. For example, they contended that since the war started on the 38th parallel it should end there. When their arguments failed them they took refuge in vituperation, insults, and rage. You could always tell their estimate of the progress they were making from the amount of obnoxious propaganda that blared forth on the Communist radio and in their press. When they were not doing so well it intensified. I presume this was their idea of putting pressure on their opponents.

Stalling for Time

Finally the Communists had to accept the fact that no amount of vituperation or rage was going to make us agree to the 38th parallel. In order to gain time to figure out their next move they created a fake incident on August 22, charged us with a violation of the Conference neutral zone and then recessed the talks. This recess lasted for two months. During this period the Eighth Army launched a number of limited offensives that were costly in territory for the enemy. At the same time it was announced that as the battle line moved north so would the demarcation line. The enemy began to see the light and requested a resumption of the talks. At General [Matthew] Ridgway's insistence they also accepted a new conference site at Panmunjom, a site more acceptable to us than Kaesong [the old Korean capital that, when originally chosen, sat between the two armies. As that war progressed and the lines shifted, Kaesong ended up behind the U.S. front line.]

When the talks were resumed on October 25, we had heard the last of the 38th parallel. The enemy had come around to our idea that the battle line should be the basis for the demilitarized zone. However there was an important difference. The Communists wanted to fix the *then* existing battle line as the FINAL demarcation line between both sides. Their strategy was obvious. If the line were fixed, once and for all, there would be no reason for the Eighth Army to push them further north because we would have to give them back the territory we had gained when and if an armistice was signed. In short, the Communists wanted a *de facto* cease-fire then and there as a relief from the Eighth Army's pressure. But we insisted that the demarcation line be the battle line as of the time of the signing of the armistice. We realized if the line were fixed permanently before completion of the negotiations the Communists could stall to their hearts content over the remaining items of the agenda. General Ridgway and the delegation felt very strongly that this was a situation calling for more steel and less silk. We felt certain the Communists would eventually give in on this point, thus assuring us of the retention of the negotiating initiative and of continuing pressure by the Eighth Army.

However, orders came through to agree to the then existing battle line as a provisional demarcation line with a thirty-day time limit. This was done in a plenary session on November 27. Presumably the decision had been made on the basis that it would serve as an incentive for the Communists to show good faith by speeding up agreement on honorable and equitable terms. Instead of showing good faith they dragged their feet at every opportunity and used the thirty days of grace to dig in and stabilize their battle line.

In retrospect, I believe this was the turning point of the Armistice Conference, and a principal reason progress slowed to a snail's pace from then on. In demonstrating our own good faith we lost the initiative, never to regain it. We were no longer negotiating from a position of strength but from a position of military stalemate. And slowly before our eyes that which we wanted most to avoid began to happen—the balance of military advantages began to shift in favor of the enemy. The end of the thirty-day time limit was just another date on the calendar. No one wanted to launch another ground offensive because the psychological handicap would be too large to overcome. The impetus was gone. And if the UNC did launch an offensive it would be with the foreknowledge that the price would be extremely high because of the time the enemy had been given to prepare.

Action Spoke Louder than Words

Rather late, and yet comparatively early, in our efforts to end the war, we had to learn that in negotiating with the Communists there is no substitute for the imperative logic of military pressure. In other words, we learned that progress in negotiating with them is in direct proportion to the degree of military pressure applied.

In order that you may better understand why it is so difficult to do business with the Communists, I want to tell you at this point something of what we learned about their personality during the debates on the demilitarized zone. I have already told you how they take refuge in vituperation, rage and insults when their arguments fail them.

One of their most noticeable characteristics is a deep feeling of inferiority. We ran into it at every turn. One day [North Korean Lt. General] General Nam Il, their senior delegate, called attention to the fact that I had spoken for seventy minutes. The next day, not to be outdone, he spoke for 110 minutes. On the first day of the Conference we placed a small standard with the United Nations flag in the center of the table. When we returned from a recess we found a North Korean flag flying from a standard several inches taller than ours. The day after I drove to Panmunjom for the first time in an Army Chevrolet sedan, Nam Il, who had always ridden in a jeep before, arrived in a captured

Chrysler. They could never match us with helicopters, however, and I think that really bothered them. . . .

Another characteristic was their apparent lack of latitude in negotiating. They were mere puppets who were bound hand and foot by the explicit instructions of their superiors. The vehemence with which they attempted to carry out instructions was no doubt inspired by the instinct of self-preservation. Presumably, they were afraid of their necks if they failed. They never gave an immediate definite answer to any of our proposals no matter how minor. Instead they would invariably say: "We will study your proposition and let you know later." Judging from the time it took to get an answer we could generally guess whether the matter was referred to Peiping or Moscow for a decision. Naturally this was very time-consuming. Incidentally it soon became evident that the Chinese were the real bosses at the Conference table. Nam Il never said anything of importance without first getting the nod from General Hsieh Fang, one of the two Chinese members of the opposing delegation and the smartest one of the lot. . . .

The Irreconcilable Prisoner of War Issue

In order to speed up the snail's pace progress, I proposed simultaneous discussions by two different sub-delegations on this item and the next item of the agenda, namely: "Arrangements pertaining to Prisoners of War." The Communists, of course, protested but in the end reluctantly agreed and on December 11, 1951, we began the long-drawn-out negotiations on the prisoner question.

At the initial meeting of the sub-delegation handling the POW [prisoner of war] question the Communists made another one of their malevolently naive suggestions. They said: "In order to reach a quick agreement on this item of the agenda we think it best to release all prisoners of war after the armistice and let them go home soon." This was a little too simple for us. What did the Communists mean when they said all? Did they mean only the 110 prisoners they had reported to Geneva? Or did they mean roughly

70,000 they had boasted over the radio as having captured during the first nine months of the war? We had no means of knowing and they refused to tell us. They wanted us to agree to the principle of an all for all exchange of prisoners before they would exchange lists of names. Of course, we refused to buy a pig in a poke. We insisted on an exchange of lists of prisoners' names so we would know what we were talking about.

Finally our sub-delegation wore them down and they agreed to exchange the lists of names. We handed them a list containing about 132,000 names and they handed us one containing only 11,559. Their list included only 3,198 U.S. personnel or hardly 27 percent of the number of U.S. personnel missing in action.

We were, of course, dumbfounded at the paucity of the list handed us. When we demanded an explanation as to what had happened to the large number of prisoners they boasted as having captured they blandly said that they had died or had been released at the front and were home leading peaceful lives. What they probably meant was that more than 50,000 captured South Korean soldiers had been impressed into their armies.

The details of what went on during the next several months on this prisoner of war question are numerous and involved. Let me summarize by saying that the UNC proposed initially to return to the Communists every one we held who wanted to go back to their side. In other words we proposed the principle of voluntary repatriation. As you know, there had been thousands in our POW camps who had already indicated they would rather die than go back to their former masters. Subsequently we modified our position to one of no forced repatriation, that is, only those who would forcibly resist returning to Communist control would be permitted to stay on our side.

Forced Repatriation

In the long weeks and months of debate, the Communists presented only two objections to voluntary repatriation.

They claimed it was contrary to the Geneva Conventions and that it was a "sinister scheme" to "forcibly detain large numbers of prisoners of war." It was very odd to hear the Communists piously quoting from the Geneva Conventions after they had systematically and deliberately broken every rule in the book during the war.

The debate wore on. Finally in the latter part of March the Communists indicated they would be willing to seek a solution to the prisoner question on the basis of "round numbers" to be returned. The implication was that if a sufficient number of people held by us elected to go north, or indicated they would not forcibly resist going north, the Communists would accept the figure. We pointed out that the only way to arrive at such a "round number" would be to screen the prisoners the UNC had in custody and thus determine their attitudes. When the Communists tacitly agreed on April 4 the screening operation was set in motion. . . .

To the unqualified amazement of everyone at our base camp the screening of prisoners revealed that only an estimated 70,000 persons in our custody would return to the Communist side without the application of force. When this figure was presented to the Communists they replied with a torrent of vituperation while their propaganda machine shifted into high gear. The die was cast. The time had come for a showdown. . . .

I presented a package proposal embodying our final effort to reach agreement. This compromise solution, originated in Washington, was incorporated in the draft of an entire armistice agreement consisting of sixty-two paragraphs. The crux of the solution was that we agreed to omit the paragraph prohibiting the construction of military airfields during an armistice provided the Communists would give in on the prisoner of war issue. . . .

I pointed out to Nam Il that our offer would have to be accepted in toto or rejected in toto. It was not subject to piecemeal negotiation—in fact it was not subject to negotiation at all. After ten long months we had reached the end of the line. It gave me a feeling of relief and satisfaction, I can assure you, to be able to lay our final offer to the table. . . .

My last two memorable weeks at Panmunjom convinced me that the Communists were not interested in reaching a fair and humanitarian solution to the prisoner of war question. I say this because of their vicious propaganda statements. Replete with distortions and falsehoods, these statements were designed solely to lend credibility to their claim that the UNC was forcibly detaining their people. The statements were directed almost entirely to the emotions of the Communist world and not to the intelligence of their opponents. The Communists just could not face or accept the fact that large numbers of their people including their so-called volunteers would rather die than return to Communist control. Furthermore, the principle of voluntary repatriation symbolized the fundamental difference between the free world and the Communist world. As you know in the free world the individual counts for everything; in the Communist world the individual counts for nothing and the state for everything. There is no such thing as individual free choice in the Communist world. . . .

Peace Through the Application of Power
The net result of my ten months of meeting with the Communists convinces me beyond the shadow of a doubt that in dealing with them there is no substitute for power. As I have said publicly before, and as I say again, the only way to negotiate with them is through patience and unmistakable firmness backed up by military force and the willingness to use that force. Nothing else makes sense to the Communist mind. They are not impressed by logic nor are they remotely concerned with morality. Their guiding precept is that the end justifies the means. The only arguments they understand are our Army, Navy, and Air Force. The only factor that impresses them is our military power in being. And the only real persuader we have is our willingness to use that power. It is idle and foolish to think otherwise; in fact, it may be suicidal from the national standpoint.

The Chinese Perspective of the Peace Process

Chai Chengwen

Major General Chai Chengwen was head of the Chinese military operations in Korea from August 1950 to January 1955. He also represented the Chinese People's Volunteer Force at the truce talks. The following selection is taken from his memoirs. In it, he discusses how the Chinese delegates viewed their American counterparts as well as the issues that were posed by both sides. Although it was written well after the end of the Korean War, it still provides an interesting contrast to the observations made by Vice Admiral C. Turner Joy.

In the afternoon of June 30, 1951, Ridgway appointed Vice Adm. C. Turner Joy, commander of the U.S. Naval Forces Far East, as his chief representative in the negotiations. Joy proved himself to be a steadfast man with a sure hand at the truce-talks table. His negotiating skills left a deep impression on several Chinese–North Korean delegation members. However, as a professional military officer, Joy could do no more than follow the instructions of [President Harry S.] Truman, Secretary of State Dean Acheson, and Ridgway. It was quite obvious that at times his ideas differed from his superiors' intentions. The negotiations were broken off several times by the American delegation, not because of Joy's ideas but because of instructions that he received from his superiors.

After Joy accepted the appointment as the chief representative, he recommended his own deputy chief of staff,

Xiaobing Li, Allan R. Millett, and Bin Yu, translators and editors, *Mao's Generals Remember Korea*. Lawrence: University Press of Kansas, 2001. Copyright © 2001 by University Press of Kansas. Reproduced by permission.

Rear Adm. Arleigh A. Burke, to be the [naval] representative at the talks. The commander of the U.S. Far East Air Forces recommended his deputy commander, Maj. Gen. Lawrence C. Craigie, as a representative. Among the others, Commander of the U.S. Eighth Army James Van Fleet recommended his deputy chief of staff, Maj. Gen. Henry I. Hodes, and the commander of the South Korean I Corps, Maj. Gen. Paik Sun Yup, as representatives. These nominations were all approved by General Ridgway.

General Craigie had good analytical skills and was eloquent. General Hodes, who was once assistant commander of the U.S. Seventh Infantry Division, was a rather plain and straightforward man, always with a cigar dangling from his lips. Admiral Burke was "very intelligent and talented," according to Joy. Yet we did not see these qualities during the process of the truce talks.

The American delegation also included a group of officers and civilian officials from the offices of the Joint Chiefs of Staff, State Department, and Ridgway's headquarters in Japan who made up a think tank for their negotiating team. Among them were naval Capt. Henry M. Briggs, an officer with a ready pen whom Joy transferred from the Headquarters of the U.S. Navy to the negotiations as the secretary of the American delegation. Col. Donald H. Galloway from the U.S. Army was responsible for its administrative work. Col. Andrew J. Kinney from the U.S. Air Force, Col. James C. Murray from the U.S. Marine Corps, and Lt. Col. Lee Soo Young of South Korea were the liaison officers.

During the later negotiations, Colonel Kinney seemed frivolous and arrogant and liked to make caustic remarks. Colonel Murray impressed us as being well educated and refined in his manners. There sometimes appeared to be several civilian officials sitting near the negotiation table who seemed to have come from the State Department. The high-ranking Korean officers, like Paik Sun Yup and Lee Hyun Gun, were young, with a training background in the U.S. Army. They, however, had merely an ornamental function in the delegation. For instance, Paik Sun Yup was sitting to the right of Joy who, nevertheless, often skipped over him to pass notes to Hodes for advice. Lee was even more ignored by the Americans. It happened once that during a recess, he was left alone in our area by his fellow delegation members, which made him extremely nervous. The Chinese–North Korean delegation sent Comrade Bi Jilong [Chinese delegate] to invite Lee to rest in our rooms and eat a meal with us. We had to call the other side and ask them to come over to pick him up.

In an apple orchard near Munsan, south of the Imjin River, the U.S. Eighth Army set up a tent camp for the American delegation. When the meetings were adjourned, they lived there unless the recess was very long. On the eve of the Korean truce negotiations, July 9, 1951, General Ridgway, commander of the UN Forces, flew from Tokyo to Seoul with the American delegation. On the morning of July 10, the delegation took helicopters to Munsan. Ridgway came to see the delegates off.

Both Sides Understandably Cautious

According to what we found out later, the Americans in the delegation expected early success in the truce discussions. In his memoirs, Joy admitted that he thought at the beginning of the talks that two months would be enough time to bring an end to the war. But even as the number one post–World War II power in the world, the United States had not won the war on the Korean battlefield. The American government had to send [Joy] to an area under our control to negotiate peace as the representative of the commander of the UN Forces. This fact itself put him and his delegation under heavy psychological pressure. Although Washington and Ridgway had given him detailed instructions, Joy had no idea what the adversary would look like, what kind of situations he would face, and how he could best deal with his counterparts at the talks. These circumstances made him uneasy, and he had to look carefully before taking each step. Just as Li Kenong [head of the Chinese and North Korean delegation] had asked us, Joy asked his delegation members to "watch closely every move made by the other side's representatives."

Kaesong [Communist-held town south of the Thirty-Eighth Parallel] was an ancient capital of the Koryo Dynasty between 918 and 1329. The people on the Korean peninsula, who had suffered much in the whirlpool of the war, were now watching the truce negotiations there. The Chinese and American peoples, as well as the peace-loving peoples of the whole world, were also watching.

Kaesong had a lot of sunshine on July 10, something rare for the Korean summer season. Men and women, old and young, indeed the entire population of the town, revealed some joy in the midst of concerns and doubts. Roads and streets were cleaned up to receive the delegation from the other side.

The PRC [People's Republic of China]–DPRK [Democratic People's Republic of Korea] delegation set up a liaison station at Panmunjom, which is located outside Kaesong on the bank of the Sachon River. Our security officers, with some translators, were sent out by our delegation to receive the other delegation. Soldiers of the NKPA and the CPVF [Chinese People's Volunteer Forces] in charge of security had received rigorous instructions to guard their posts carefully in order to guarantee the safety of the representatives from the other side. All the participating members of the PRC–DPRK delegation gathered a half hour in advance. Delegates from the CPVF put on dark green uniforms. On the left side of their chests, red ribbons read in Korean and Chinese "Sino-Korean Delegation for Truce Negotiations."

At eight o'clock the motorcade of jeeps and trucks carrying some delegation members from the other side departed from Munsan. Following the designated roads across the Imjin River, they headed to the Panmunjom bridge on the Sachon River. From there our security officers led the way so they could rest in the white pavilion located on the outskirts of Kaesong. At 9:00 A.M. two helicopters carrying

Vice Admiral Joy and some of his staff arrived on the landing site we had prepared.

At 10:00 A.M. the two delegations from both sides met in the hall of Naebongjang [tea house]. Then both delegations walked into the meeting room, sat down, and exchanged certification papers for inspection. A rectangular table covered with green woolen cloth was set up at an east-west angle in the negotiating room. On the southern side were the five representatives from the other side: Joy sat in the middle, with Paik Sun Yup and Hodes on his right-hand side and with Craigie and Burke on his left-hand side. The PRC–DPRK representatives were sitting on the northern side of the table. Nam Il sat in the middle, with Deng Hua and Xie Fang on his right-hand side and with Lee Sang Cho and Chang Pyong San on his left. Behind the representatives of both sides were staff members, translators, and recording secretaries in roughly equivalent numbers.

The Americans Take the Floor First

According to international negotiating practice, the Chinese–North Korean side should have taken the floor first, since the truce talks were held in an area under our control and especially so given that the negotiations were based on equity, without a chairman. Joy, however, raced to take the floor without waiting for our representatives to have a say.

Having stressed the importance of the negotiations, Joy said that the Korean War would continue until a cease-fire agreement took effect and that any delay in reaching an agreement would mean prolonging the war and increasing casualties. These were plain words, yet they certainly carried a threatening connotation under these particular circumstances. Before ending his speech, Joy proposed, "What we are going to talk about will be confined to purely military matters regarding the Korean territory. If you agree with me on this proposal, please sign a document right now as the first agreement of our negotiations. Would you do that?" It was really disappointing that at the first meeting that attracted the world's attention, the other side was unable to make any substantial proposition.

We ignored Joy's request. General Nam Il as our chief representative made his speech next. He pointed out that the Korean people insisted, as they had before, on ending the war as quickly as possible. For this reason, he and the PRC–DPRK delegation supported the proposition made by Jacob Malik, Soviet ambassador to the United Nations, on June 23, 1951, calling for an immediate cease-fire by both sides and a withdrawal of all troops back from the Thirty-eighth Parallel.

Nam Il then officially stated three fundamental principles. First, on the basis of a mutual agreement, both sides should simultaneously order their troops to stop military actions. He stressed that a cease-fire by both sides would not only reduce the loss of human lives and property but would also contribute the first step toward putting out the fire of war in Korea.

Second, both sides should agree to establish the Thirty-eighth Parallel as the military demarcation line. All troops should retreat ten kilometers away from it. This area between both sides then should be considered as a demilitarized zone [a neutral zone between the North and South Korean borders] for a certain time period. The civil administration of the area would be restored to the same condition prior to June 25, 1950. At the same time, negotiations between both sides on exchanges of prisoners of war should be held as soon as possible.

Third, foreign troops must withdraw from Korea as early as possible so as to put an end to the conflict permanently and settle the Korean problem peacefully. Only the withdrawal of foreign troops could provide the fundamental basis for ending the war.

Nam Il also expressed a sincere wish that the negotiations at Kaesong reach an armistice at the earliest possible time, in order to meet the needs of the peace-loving people. After his talk, General Deng Hua, representative of the CPVF, made a speech in support of Nam's viewpoints. Deng said that an important step toward a peaceful solution of the Korean problem could be taken only after we met and talked about a cease-fire on fair and reasonable grounds. A cease-fire, a temporary military demarcation line along the Thirty-eighth Parallel, and the withdrawal of all foreign troops were the conditions that the Koreans, the Chinese, and the people of the world were wishing and waiting for. Nam's three principles were fully supported by the Chinese Volunteers, Deng emphasized.

The Chinese and North Korean governments had already made an agreement that Nam Il would be the key speaker representing the Chinese–North Korean side. Deng's speech was arranged specifically just for the first day, because the people of the entire world were fully aware that the Americans were expecting to hear China's position at the truce negotiations. If the representatives of the CPVF had articulated nothing, not only would the Americans not have confidence at Kaesong but also the peace-wishing people of the world would not be satisfied.

The Americans Insist on Their Own Points

Originally, the PRC–DPRK delegation thought that it would save a lot of time in such urgent talks if both sides first put their cards on the table, found similarities in their positions, and then discussed their differences item by item. We had sufficient reasons for such an approach because there existed many common points and similar views in the speech made by George Kennan [U.S. state department diplomat] and the declaration of Jacob Malik at the United Nations.

Such, however, was not the case at Kaesong. After Nam's and Deng's speeches, the other side proposed nine items for immediate negotiations:

1. Pass an agenda for the talks.
2. Identify the locations of prisoners' camps on both sides. Give permission to the International Committee of the Red Cross to visit camps.
3. Limit discussions and negotiations at the talks only to military matters on the Korean territory.
4. Stop all hostile actions and military movements be-

tween both sides' armed forces. Discuss clauses to guarantee that no such military actions and movements would take place again in the future.

5. Determine a demilitarized zone in Korea.
6. Discuss the organization, authority, and responsibilities of a supervising commission for the truce in Korea.
7. Discuss principles for establishing a military observation group that would conduct observations in Korea under the supervising commission of the Korean Armistice.
8. Decide the organization and responsibilities of the above group.
9. Make arrangements for prisoners of the Korean War.

At the lunch recess, the members of the PRC–DPRK delegation studied the wording of the other side's proposals. It seemed to us that the first item concerned only the procedure of the negotiations. The second item seemed to be a needless, rigid insertion because there was no need to talk about POW camp visits by the Red Cross International Committee at the truce negotiations. The third item was evidently added unnecessarily. Regarding the scope of the talks, although Kennan had proposed [to Malik] that negotiations for an armistice be an independent issue, the mere definition of military matters would itself create endless debate in the negotiations.

Our guess about the real intention behind the proposal of these two items was that the Americans were afraid of getting involved in the debate concerning the question of Taiwan and the issue of a PRC seat in the UN, or perhaps they wanted to instigate conflict between the International Committee of the Red Cross and the PRC–DPRK delegation at the talks. Among the other proposals, the fourth and fifth items were actually at the core of the issue. However, the other side did not raise the real question about how to define a demilitarized zone. Without military boundaries, there would be no basis for determining such a zone. The sixth, seventh, and eighth items dealt with the supervision of an armistice, that is, how to guarantee that no more military actions would take place in the future. The last item was about the POWs.

In fact, the substance of the nine items was already included in the three principles proposed by Nam. To our regret, the other side did not mention even a word about withdrawing foreign troops, nor did it mention anything about retreating from the Thirty-eighth Parallel. Those were the key issues that needed discussion and solutions. It was apparent that the Americans had already modified their stand at the talks. Li Kenong said that the Americans no longer seemed to be in a hurry to reach an armistice as much as they had been when Kennan wanted to meet Malik.

We Propose Our Own Points

Since the negotiations were based on equal status between both sides, it would have been inappropriate for us to oppose the other side's agenda for discussions. That afternoon the Chinese–North Korean side also proposed five items for discussion:

1. Pass the agenda for the negotiations.
2. Use the Thirty-eighth Parallel as the military demarcation line for the purpose of a cease-fire on both sides. Establish a nonmilitary zone. These measures are the basic foundation for the armistice.
3. Withdraw all foreign armed forces from Korea.
4. Define concrete, specific measures to enforce the cease-fire.
5. Make arrangements for the prisoners of war.

Each speech delivered at the meeting was translated into two languages—ours into Korean and English, theirs into Korean and Chinese. The two-language translations, in fact, worked toward the advantage of both sides, because the time required by the translations could be used to think and even discuss how to reply to the questions from the other side.

Nonetheless, on several occasions, possibly because of nervousness or negligence, after [the American delegation's interpreter] Richard Underwood translated Joy's words into Korean, the vice admiral kept going on with his speech without waiting for the Chinese translation by Kenneth Wu [in the American delegation]. This was corrected only after the PRC–DPRK delegation complained about it.

There was no joint record-keeping or note-taking team. Each side took notes for itself. The other side was using a stenographic machine and thus seemed at some ease, while we, using pens, were pressured by haste. We tried to keep the records of the other side's speeches in English since Underwood did not speak Korean very well, nor did Wu speak Chinese well.

Underwood's father was an American missionary in Korea. Although Underwood grew up in South Korea, his Korean was imprecise, and he was not proficient enough as an interpreter for negotiations. However, he set high standards for himself. In the long and tense process of translation, Underwood even kept an accurate record of his smoking by jotting down in his pocket-size notebook the exact time he had a cigarette.

Kenneth Wu was a young and capable Chinese-American. He had a sense of justice. His language ability improved quickly during the process of the negotiations, and the Chinese–North Korean delegation members were well disposed toward him. Yet his Chinese was underqualified for the needs of the negotiations. For example, he once translated "running into someone" as "two cars run into each other on the road." Particularly when his speakers were logically inconsistent in the debates, Wu reluctantly did his job and then looked at the Chinese representatives with an expression of resignation.

The United States Prevented a Negotiated Peace

Kim Il Sung

Kim Il Sung was a Korean revolutionary who fought against the Japanese occupation in Korea and China. At the end of World War II, the Soviet Union formed the Democratic People's Republic in North Korea and installed Sung as its premier. One of the first things Sung did was convince Soviet leader Joseph Stalin that he could successfully invade South Korea. But even with Soviet and Chinese support, the war ended in a stalemate with heavy losses for both sides. Sung's plans to unify Korea under communism were thwarted by U.S./UN intervention. In the following excerpt, Sung criticizes the United States for keeping Korea divided, but he asserts that the North Koreans emerged as the victors of the Korean War.

The present Sixth Plenary Meeting of the Central Committee of our Party is convened under the new situation created in our country following the signing of the Armistice Agreement.

The heroic struggle waged by the Korean people for three years in defence of the country's freedom and independence against the US imperialist armed invaders ended in victory for us. The US imperialist aggressors suffered an ignominious defeat in their military adventure to turn our country into their colony and enslave the Korean people. The enemy was compelled to sign the Armistice Agreement owing to his irretrievable military, political and moral defeat in the Ko-

Kim Il Sung, *Kim Il Sung: For the Independent, Peaceful Reunification of the Country*. Pyongyang, Korea: Foreign Languages Publishing House, 1976.

rean war, and thanks to the tenacious and patient efforts of the Korean and Chinese peoples to restore peace in Korea and to the public opinion and pressure of the peace-loving peoples of the world. Thus, the Korean people won a glorious victory in their Fatherland Liberation War.

In this sacred war our Workers' Party [Communist] members fought courageously in the forefront of the entire Korean people.

Our Workers' Party played the role of the pivot and organizer in the People's Army, and performed a great function in strengthening it. Members of the Workers' Party in the People's Army always bore the brunt of battles in any offensive or defensive, any mountain or field operation, courageously waging hand-to-hand fights. Our Party members constituted the backbone and acted as models in the People's Army.

Our Workers' Party members in the rear surmounted all hardships and difficulties in the face of barbarous enemy bombing under difficult wartime conditions; they restored and developed factories and mines, ensured railway transport, and steadily increased production in farming and fishing villages. Our Workers' Party members, in factories built underground, kept up munitions production for the front; assured the transport of war supplies satisfactorily by running trains and trucks even on dark nights and in defiance of the enemy's bombings; continued fishing in face of frenzied enemy warships; and ploughed and sowed with camouflaged oxen.

We Did Not Yield

During the enemy's occupation, our Party members did not yield to the enemy at all, but fought and were victorious in guerrilla warfare, holding high the banner of the Republic to the end. In the enemy's POW [prisoner of war] camps, too, despite all sorts of persecutions and barbarous massacre by the enemy, our Party members never gave in but defended to the last their honour as Workers' Party members as well as the banner of our Republic.

Who but members of our Workers' Party could have ever organized so heroic a struggle at the front and in the rear? There is no doubt that if the members of the Workers' Party had not heroically fought at the head of all the popular masses, we would have failed to win, and would have been doomed to colonial slavery to the US imperialists.

Today the Workers' Party of Korea, through its devoted, heroic struggle, has proved itself a reliable vanguard to which the Korean people can entrust their destiny and future without hesitation; it represents the wisdom and glory of the Korean people. Thus, our Party, in the struggle for safeguarding the country's freedom and independence and for a happier and more resplendent future of the people, has been strengthened and developed into a revolutionary party armed with all-conquering Marxist-Leninist theory. In the Fatherland Liberation War, our Party, as member of the "shock force" of the international working-class movement, made a tremendous contribution to the consolidation of the camp of democracy and socialism and to the safeguarding of world peace.

I feel a boundless pride at the fact that I, as a member of so glorious a party as the Workers' Party of Korea, share this great honour with you.

On behalf of the Sixth Plenary Meeting of the Party Central Committee, I extend warm thanks to all the functionaries and Party members in the People's Army, factories, urban communities, farming and fishing villages, on the railways, in interior service organs, self-defence corps, garrison troops, Party and state organs, cultural institutions, and social organizations.

Also, in the name of the Sixth Plenary Meeting of the Party Central Committee, I express warm gratitude to the members of all the democratic political parties and people of all walks of life who, shoulder to shoulder with our Party members, fought actively for the freedom and independence of the country against the US imperialist armed invaders.

And I extend warm gratitude and congratulations to the men and officers of the Chinese People's Volunteers who aided us in our struggle for the freedom and independence of our country at the cost of their blood.

I express warm gratitude to the peoples of the great Soviet Union, China and other People's Democracies, as well as to their Communist and Workers' Parties, for the continuous and unselfish aid they gave us during the period of peaceful construction and especially during the war.

I extend profound thanks to good-minded people all over the world for rendering active support and encouragement to the sacred cause of us Korean people.

On the Armistice and the Question of the Country's Reunification

The armistice signifies a great victory for us. Though the armistice did not bring complete peace to Korea, the conclusion of the Armistice Agreement marked an initial step towards the peaceful settlement of the Korean issue, a first exemplary contribution to the relaxation of international tension. By concluding the Armistice Agreement, we have come to open up the possibilities for the peaceful settlement of the question of our country's reunification.

It is wrong to think, as some comrades do, that war might soon break out again and that peaceful construction could not be undertaken because the armistice does not mean a complete peace. It is likewise a wrong tendency to be indolent, lax and self-contented, thinking that an end has been put to war and complete peace is ensured in our country. The point is to consolidate the victory embodied in the armistice, which we have won at enormous sacrifices by going through the tribulations and calamities of war, and to struggle unremittingly for a lasting peace in Korea and the peaceful reunification of the country.

The first and foremost task confronting us in connection with the conclusion of the Armistice Agreement is to struggle persistently for a complete peaceful settlement of the question of our country at the forthcoming political conference. The basic aim of the political conference is to get all the troops of the United States and its satellite countries to withdraw from south Korea and to enable the Korean people to settle the Korean issue by themselves, and to prevent foreigners from interfering in the internal affairs of our country. We have advocated with all consistency the peaceful settlement of the Korean issue—the peaceful reunification of the country. It is quite evident that if the US imperialists had not interfered and if the Korean question had been solved in accordance with our line and claims, our country would have long ago been reunified, and our country and people would have been freed from all the sufferings and disasters resulting from the country's division. Our task is to carry our just line and claims into effect and to do everything for their realization.

Reunification Is a Korean Issue

The Korean nation is one and Korea belongs to the Koreans. The Korean question must naturally be settled by the Korean people themselves. The Korean people absolutely do not want to remain split. No aggressive force can break the desire and will of the Korean people for the reunification of their country.

The forthcoming political conference should naturally reflect and defend the just claims, desire, will and fundamental interests of the Korean people. Therefore, our people will under no circumstances tolerate, and thoroughly reject, any attempt or plot of the imperialist interventionists contrary to them.

With the political conference approaching, the US imperialists are already making a fuss behind the scenes. Notwithstanding the signing of the Armistice Agreement in which it was stipulated that the chief aim of the political conference is to discuss the question of withdrawal of foreign troops from Korea, the notorious warmonger [John Foster] Dulles US Secretary of State, concluded the so-called "ROK-US [Republic of Korea/United States] Mutual Defence Pact" with the traitor Syngman Rhee [the South Korean president]. This pact is aimed at stationing aggressive forces of the United States in south Korea indefinitely and, whenever necessary, unleashing another criminal war of aggression in

Korea, in violation of the Armistice Agreement. The "ROK-US Mutual Defence Pact" is an aggressive pact which allows US imperialism to obstruct the peaceful reunification of our country and interfere in our domestic affairs. It is a glaringly country-selling pact under which the Syngman Rhee clique sell the southern half of our country to the US bandits. To conclude such a pact at a time when the political conference is in the offing is an act hindering a reasonable solution of the Korean question at the political conference. It can be easily foreseen that they will seek to throw the political conference into confusion, resorting to all sorts of intrigues, obstructive tactics and provocations at the conference, too, just as they did during the truce talks.

We, however, must by all means fulfil the just claims and demands of the Korean people by relying on the powerful support and encouragement of the peace-loving peoples all over the world, and by the unanimous will and struggle of the Korean people, just as we did in the course of the truce talks. Thus the political conference should certainly be brought to the expected results and our country reunified peacefully without fail. To attain this goal, we must wage an unremitting struggle.

All our Party members and people should not relax their keyed-up attitude and, without slacking off in the least, should increase their revolutionary vigilance to a high degree, keep a close watch on every movement of the enemy, and be ready at all times to see through the enemy's vicious designs and frustrate them in advance.

All the Party members and the entire people should rally still more firmly around the Party Central Committee and the Government and do their utmost to increase the might of the country in every way. We have ample conditions and possibilities triumphantly to carry out this task which confronts our nation, our state and our Party.

We Must Compel the United States to Leave

Today, following the armistice, the situation in south Korea has been plunged into hopeless chaos. Antagonisms and contradictions are being further aggravated within the enemy camp, and the life of the people becomes more and more wretched. Growing and gaining in scope among the masses of the people are hatred and rebellious trends against the US imperialist aggressors and the traitorous Syngman Rhee's reactionary rule which is maintained by their bayonets. The enemy's military, political and economic crises are becoming more grave. This will no doubt provide a favourable condition for the Korean people in their struggle for the peaceful reunification of the country.

The task is to arouse to the struggle for the peaceful reunification of the country all the democratic, patriotic forces of popular masses throughout the country, rallying them around our Party and Government, and to make it possible to settle the Korean question by us Koreans by repudiating the colonial occupation policy of the US imperialist aggressors and the traitorous rule of their lackeys and by compelling the US forces of aggression to withdraw.

Politics Prevented a U.S. Victory in Korea

Mark Clark and James Van Fleet

In May 1952 U.S. Army general Mark Clark succeeded General Matthew Ridgway as commander of U.S./UN forces in Korea and inherited the job of negotiating an armistice to end the war. Clark did not relish the task since he believed UN forces could break the deadlock and defeat North Korea. But he performed his duty and signed the treaty on July 27, 1953. Shortly afterward, Clark and other military leaders were brought before an investigative Senate subcommittee to discuss what had gone wrong in Korea. The American public was dissatisfied with the seeming pointlessness of the Korean War. Politicians sought to divert the blame by putting the commanders of the war on trial before an investigative committee. The following excerpts are taken from a transcript of the Senate testimony of General Mark Clark and General James Van Fleet.

General Clark fully supported General [Douglas] MacArthur. General Clark believes that we should have and could have won; that the action required would not have precipitated world war III, that, on the contrary, we missed a golden opportunity by failing to act when the Chinese Communists intervened.

The following excerpts are from the sections of his testimony which deal with the Korean war and related matters:

... Mr. [Alva C.] CARPENTER [chief counsel and executive director]. General Clark, did you agree with General MacArthur that the enemy should not have been allowed a

Mark Clark and James Van Fleet, testimony before the Senate Committee on the Judiciary, Subcommittee to Investigate the Administration of the Internal Security Act and Other Internal Security Laws, 84th Cong., 1st sess., January 21, 1955.

sanctuary beyond the Yalu [River]?

General CLARK. Yes, sir; I agreed at the time when they came in. I think that that was the crucial day in American history in 1950 when thousands upon thousands of Chinese ostensibly picked up individual rifles because they were individually mad at the United States and came across the Yalu and killed our men. I think at that time, we should have indicated that we were at war with Red China and should have retaliated with everything we had at our disposal. . . .

Senator MCCARRAN. [Senator Pat McCarran (D-Nevada) was head of the Senate internal security subcommittee, which had investigated the administrations of Franklin Roosevelt and Harry Truman for alleged Communist influence.] Was it your judgment or is it your judgment now that, had we crossed the Yalu River at the time the Chinese came across, that might have triggered a third world war?

General CLARK. It might have; yes, sir. My own opinion is what you have asked. I do not think it would have started world war III, nor do I think, when I was in command and had I bombed the bases, which I would like to have done, and the airfields from which the enemy derived his source of power, that that would have dragged us into world war III.

I do not think you can drag the Soviets into a world war except at a time and place of their own choosing. They have been doing too well in the cold war. . . .

Senator [Herman] WELKER [of the Committee on the Judiciary]. Would you tell the committee what you were authorized to do with respect to the bombing of the bridges across the Yalu?

General CLARK. I was denied the right to bomb or destroy the bridges. . . .

[Committee] Chairman [William] JENNER. General, did you ever fight a war like this before and would you ever want to fight another one like it?

General CLARK. No, sir. . . .

Mr. CARPENTER. Do you, then, believe that the Russians would have entered the war?

General CLARK. They might have, but, in my opinion, I

do not think that would have brought them into the war. I must again reiterate that I don't think you can drag them into a war except when they think the time and place is right. I do not think it would have triggered world war III.

Chairman JENNER. [Committee member] Senator [Olin D.] Johnston.

Senator JOHNSTON. General, I have been a great advocate of bombing behind the line in Manchuria and behind the Yalu River, too. But isn't it true, also, that there are two theories: One, it might bring on a third world war, and another, held by another group, that it might not and it might end the war quickly? I believe it would end the war quickly, and I think that is your theory?

General CLARK. Yes, sir; that is mine.

Certainly there is, as I tried to point out, another side, the bringing on of world war III, and the fact that our allies were adamant against anything such as that. What they are worth, I am not in a position to decide, but those were the other considerations. . . .

Mr. CARPENTER. When our fighters are involved and when it is necessary to fight, how should we fight?

General CLARK. Once our leaders, our authorized leaders, the President and Congress, decide that fight we must, in my opinion we should fight without any holds barred whatsoever.

We should fight to win, and we should not go in for a limited war where we put our limited manpower against the unlimited hordes of Communist manpower which they are willing to expend lavishly, and do. They have no value for human life or respect for it at all.

If fight we must, let's go in there and shoot the works for victory with everything at our disposal. . . .

Chairman JENNER. You have had sufficient experience and you have testified about it here this morning. If our military are not permitted to develop a defense or to fight a war for the peace and security of our people but their strategy is diluted by political considerations of the State Department, what chance of success do we have to defend this country under the procedures that have happened in the past?

General CLARK. I don't know, sir. I am disturbed, as apparently you are, for I have felt in my own experience that there have been some influences at work someplace on important decisions that affected my decisions as a commander in the field.

I realize again that every military decision has its political counterparts, but I have felt in the past, from my feeling in my high commands, that too often were the military decisions overridden by other considerations. . . .

We Should Have Taken the Chance

Senator WELKER. General Clark, going back to the Yalu River, I will ask you, based upon your experience as a great military commander, in your opinion, had you or the commanders that you succeeded been permitted to bomb the installations, the airports, the means of making warfare across the Yalu River, would the free world have suffered any difficulty or any loss in Indochina?

General CLARK. Sir, if I had had authority to bomb the airbases north of the Yalu and the dumps and the depots from which they derived their power, I would have done so.

I feel that had we taken that courageous action together with offensive actions, amphibiously and otherwise, we would not have had the unhappy ending that I feel we had in Korea. We left, when we signed the armistice in Korea, an enemy on the 38th parallel, right where he started. True, we had stopped his immediate aggression to take over South Korea, but we left him there better trained.

We trained him how to fight. We left him there arrogant. He had made the people behind the Iron Curtain think that he had won a victory, and we left him ready and poised to strike again, as he did in Indochina.

To answer your question specifically, had we taken courageous action and a decision to win a military victory over there, I believe we would not have been confronted with the dilemma that has beset us in Indochina. . . .

The Testimony of General James Van Fleet

The general described the circumstances of his appointment to Korea in April 1951 and the frustration he experienced in being denied victory. He stated that he fully supported General of the Army MacArthur's recommendations, that we could have won in Korea, that Korea was "the right war" from all points of view, and that the fear that the Soviet would intervene was based on a terrible blunder in miscalculating the Russian intentions. General Van Fleet described his training of Republic of Korea troops and the constant rejection of his recommendations for action.

The following excerpts are from the sections of his testimony which deal with the Korean war and related matters. . . .

Mr. CARPENTER. What was your view concerning the MacArthur proposals in 1950?

General VAN FLEET. Those proposals I remember were to use the atomic weapons and bomb enemy targets in north China and Manchuria.

Mr. CARPENTER. I do not believe it was to use the atomic bomb. It was hot pursuit, to bomb the enemy sanctuaries in Manchuria and to drive through to the Yalu River?

General VAN FLEET. Of course, I was very much in accord with such views.

Mr. CARPENTER. How about his subsequent views?

General VAN FLEET. I have always subscribed to such action then and since. . . .

Mr. CARPENTER. Was Korea the wrong war in the wrong place and at the wrong time? [This quote was taken from General Omar Bradley's testimony during the MacArthur hearings.]

General VAN FLEET. Well, certainly not. I have often made a statement that it was the right war at the right place and the right time against the right enemy and with the right allies, thinking of the Koreans as a very worthy, friendly ally in whose country to fight. . . .

I believe General Bradley and General Collins, especially those two of the Joint Chiefs, were oriented entirely to

Western Europe and that they could not see a deployment of American strength in the far Pacific. They, I am sure, helped in the estimate of the situation that Russia would strike in Europe and not in Asia. That estimate of enemy's intentions, in my opinion, was one of the greatest errors we have ever made in sizing up our enemy's intentions. . . .

Mr. CARPENTER. General, you state that the aim of the Communists in Asia clearly is to bring all Asia into the Communist fold as part of a grand design for a Communist world. This is their announced objective, is it not?

General VAN FLEET. That is their announced objective, and their deeds are in line with it.

Senator JOHNSTON. Summing up your statement, I believe you would say this was a war fought by the military but guided by the State Department; is that right?

General VAN FLEET. That is correct. The policy was set by the State Department. I would assume they would consult certain allies, that the military would be consulted. But I believe our military was very much oriented to Europe. They went along very readily with a weak policy.

Senator JOHNSTON. I agree with you thoroughly, and I think I expressed my feelings in the matter in October 1950, in Los Angeles, in a speech that I made there. . . .

General VAN FLEET. I might say just a word more, using the map, about this being the right war and the right place.

Chairman JENNER. You may go to the map, and there is a microphone, General, that you may speak into.

General VAN FLEET. On the map you have Red China and Korea. For the Red Chinese to maintain an effort in Korea they had a single rail line along the coast through north China, running up into Manchuria; and then south across the border; at which time they came under the fire of our Air Force for 200 miles thereafter south to the battlelines, across the middle of the peninsula. That is a long supply line, a very difficult supply line. And for the Chinese to assemble and to move and support in action an army of nearly a million men halfway down this peninsula, the last 200 miles under attack, is a tremendous undertaking; which places them at a great disadvantage.

In addition, supplies from Russia, which were considerable, had to come a long distance across Siberia, by rail line, into Vladivostok and then along a much longer rail line along the Korean coast, which was under the constant fire of our Navy and air. They were paying a very heavy price to maintain a war at a point of great disadvantage to them.

The reverse of that is true of the American forces. We were supplied by water, and some air, through Japan, to Korea. We had command of the water and the air. We had, and still have, unexcelled bases in Japan and Korea for redeployment. And to maintain an expeditionary force overseas and sustain it in battle, you must have large bases.

There are only two places in the world where such conditions exist outside of the United States. One is England and the other is Japan. We had a base here, Japan, fully at our disposal, to do as we pleased about it; unexcelled harbors and repair facilities and fields.

We had the tremendous skill of the Japanese industrial nation, employed as civilians, to help us prosecute that war. It could not possibly be made or altered any better. We had the flank protected by our Navy, and all this base here to destroy a Red Chinese Army far from home, well out on the limb, and in great difficulty all the time—a beautiful opportunity for victory. . . .

Chairman JENNER. General, have you ever wondered why the experts, who must have known what you pointed out, were so blind?

General VAN FLEET. I can't figure that out, Mr. Chairman. . . .

Defeated by Our Own Limited War

Chairman JENNER. General, did you ever stop to wonder why the most powerful, the richest Nation in the world, engaged in a war that we were supposed to win, would put a limitation ceiling upon the troops of a country that our boys were defending, fighting for?

General VAN FLEET. It seemed absurb since [it was] a war

that they were willing to fight—as a matter of fact, President Rhee, bless him, would often inspect with me new arrivals of American units, and with tears in his eyes would say, "General, I don't like to see your little American boys come over here so far from home and fight in this country for us; we have lots of manpower; we will do the fighting. Just give use the weapons and the training.". . .

Mr. CARPENTER. Do you believe that the Chinese Communists would have crossed the Yalu without assurance that our military action would be limited?

General VAN FLEET. No; he would not have entered Korea if he did not feel safe from attack in north China and Manchuria.

Mr. CARPENTER. He felt pretty secure, did he not?

General VAN FLEET. I am sure he must have, or he would have been foolish to have entered Korea.

Mr. CARPENTER. Have you ever speculated as to the source of this assurance?

General VAN FLEET. I have no evidence on where he would be assured.

Chairman JENNER. General, we are looking for the "theys."

General VAN FLEET. I merely have a guess that he would get it through some embassy source in Peiping [now known as Beijing].

Military Force Must Be Used to Force Negotiations

Henry A. Kissinger

One of the biggest problems facing the United States during the Korean War was the lack of a suitable doctrine. Korea was a different kind of war than the United States had fought in the past. It was also the nation's first armed conflict during the nuclear age, which meant the outdated doctrine of "total victory" at all costs risked the possibility of another world war. The following excerpt is taken from a book that statesman Henry A. Kissinger worked on at Harvard University with a panel of foreign policy experts. In it Kissinger stresses the importance of the limited war, which he defines as "an attempt to affect the opponent's will, not to crush it." He contends that if the United States had established this doctrine in the beginning and used unrelenting military advantage to force the enemy to concede, the Korean War could have ended sooner.

Kissinger became the fifty-sixth secretary of state and was appointed assistant to the president for national security. He was instrumental in shaping U.S. foreign policy through two presidential terms and won the Nobel Peace Prize for his role in ending the Vietnam War.

When reality clashes with our expectations of it, frustration is the inevitable consequence. For Korea caught us completely unprepared not only militarily but above all in doctrine. Our strategic thinking had defined but two causes

Henry A. Kissinger, *Nuclear Weapons and Foreign Policy*. New York: Harper & Brothers, 1957. Copyright © 1957 by Council on Foreign Relations, Inc. Reproduced by permission.

of war: a surprise attack on the continental United States and military aggression against Western Europe. It had foreseen all-out war as the only solution, and it had relied on our industrial potential, backed by strategic air power, as the means to victory. Secretary [of State Dean] Acheson's speech of January 12, 1950, which excluded Korea from our defensive perimeter, was no more than an application of fundamental United States strategy, no different in content and almost identical in language with a statement made by General Douglas MacArthur nine months previously. In an all-out war with the U.S.S.R. Korea was indeed outside our defensive perimeter, and its fate would depend on the outcome of a struggle fought in other theaters. As a result, the Korean war fitted no category of our strategic thought. It was not initiated by a surprise attack against the United States, nor directed against Europe, nor did it involve the U.S.S.R. It was a war to which an all-out strategy seemed peculiarly unsuited. It has been remarked more than once that had the Korean war not actually taken place, we would never have believed that it could have.

We Were Forced to Improvise a New Strategy

It was a courageous decision to resist an aggression so totally at variance with all previous planning. The penalty we paid for the one-sidedness of our doctrine, however, was the necessity for improvising a new strategy under the pressure of events, as well as a growing difficulty in harmonizing our political and military objectives. Throughout the Korean war we were inhibited by the consciousness that this was not the war for which we had prepared. The result was an endless conflict between the commanders who, being responsible for fighting the war, sought to apply literally the doctrine that victory means crushing the enemy, and the responsible officials in Washington who, in the light of their preconceptions and the global nature of their responsibilities, could only consider the Korean war a strategic diversion or a deliberate feint on the part of the adversary.

Differing Points of View

It would be a mistake, however, to consider the controversies produced by the Korean war as a dispute about the efficacy of an all-out strategy. On the contrary, both advocates and opponents of a greater effort in Korea agreed that war, by its nature, was an all-out struggle that could be won only by crushing the enemy totally. Where they differed was not in their notion of the nature of war, but in their interpretation of the significance of the Korean war. MacArthur advocated a showdown in the Far East and specifically with China. His critics believed we must conserve our strength for a possibly imminent all-out test with the U.S.S.R. and specifically over Europe. To MacArthur the Korean war was frustration because it was not enough of a war in terms of our concept of war; to his opponents because it was too big a war in terms of the strategy on which they had built their defense plans. The dispute over the Korean war was, therefore, less a conflict over the nature of strategy than a disagreement over the *area* in which it could best be applied.

MacArthur was only expressing accepted doctrine when he asserted that "the general definition which for many decades has been accepted was that war was the ultimate process of politics; that when all other political means failed, you then go to force; and when you do that, the balance of control . . . the main interest involved . . . is the control of the military. . . . I do unquestionably state that when men become locked in battle, that there should be no artifice under the name of politics, which should . . . decrease their chances for winning. . . ." Precisely because they accepted this notion of war, MacArthur's opponents sought to keep the Korean war to the smallest proportions and to reserve our strength for the "real" test which by definition had to involve the Soviet Union: ". . . enlargement of the war in Korea to include Red China, would probably delight the [Soviet] Kremlin more than anything else we could do," argued General [Omar] Bradley [chairman of the Joint Chiefs of Staff]. "It would necessarily tie down

... our sea power and our air power. ... in an area that is not the critical strategic prize. Red China is not the powerful nation seeking to dominate the world. Frankly, in the opinion of the Joint Chiefs of Staff, this strategy would involve us in the wrong war, at the wrong place, at the wrong time, and with the wrong enemy."

The literalness of our notion of power is well expressed in our certainty that a war *against* the U.S.S.R. must necessarily take the form of a battle *with* the U.S.S.R., probably over Europe. This was the real bone of contention between MacArthur and his opponents, and it was also reflected in their disputes over the nature of preparedness. "You have got a war on your hands," MacArthur maintained, "and you can't just say, 'Let that war go on indefinitely while I prepare for some other war.' ... Does your global plan for defense of this United States ... consist of permitting war indefinitely to go on in the Pacific? ... If you are not going to bring the war to a decisive conclusion, what does the preparedness mean?" The difficulty was, of course, that it was precisely the global nature of our defense plans which left us unprepared for the challenges of the Korean war. The assumption behind our military planning had been that our wars would be fought against a principal enemy and a major challenge, but that our forces-in-being need only be powerful enough to gain us the time to mobilize our industrial potential. This doctrine presupposed two related contingencies: that other powers would bear the initial brunt of aggression and that the threat would be unambiguous.

We Need to Develop a New Doctrine
But in the aftermath of World War II, this doctrine was no longer adequate to the situation because the smaller states had lost either the strength or the will to resist by themselves. Since their ability to resist aggression had now come to depend on our willingness to commit our forces at the very beginning of any war and their decision to resist at all depended more and more on their confidence in our ability to act at once, our forces-in-being would have to be strong

enough to absorb the first blows and to strike back effectively without delay. The quandary presented by a limited war turned out to be that its challenge was either not made by a principal enemy or that it did appear as an all-out challenge. In Korea the opponent was first a satellite of the third order and then Communist China. The attack was directed not against us or our installations, but against a remote area from which we had withdrawn our troops scarcely a year before. In such a situation, it is little wonder that our preoccupation with an all-out strategy caused us to consider the Korean war as an aberration and a strategic diversion.

The notion of all-out war against a principal enemy coupled with the reliance on "purely" military considerations exaggerated the inherent conservatism of our strategic planning. It is almost axiomatic that military planners are never satisfied with their "readiness." War always has an element of uncertainty, because victory depends not only on the power available but on the manner in which the factors of power are combined. Within limits, superior leadership and doctrine can compensate for inferior resources. It is the temptation of military planning to seek to escape this element of uncertainty by assembling overwhelmingly preponderant force, to substitute power for conception. But it is difficult to assemble overwhelming force against a major enemy in peacetime, particularly while relying on a defensive strategy which concedes the first blow to the adversary. For, by definition almost, the opponent will not strike the first blow if the force arrayed against him appears to him to be overwhelming. Reliance on "purely" military considerations can, therefore, only heighten the conviction of the military planners that they are not "ready" and will induce them, in all situations short of a direct attack on the United States, to advocate postponing a showdown to a more propitious moment. "We feel that we are not in the best position to meet a global war," said General Bradley. ". . . We would like very much to avoid a war at this time, not only as to our own readiness, but the longer you can avoid a war the better chance you have of avoiding it altogether. . . ." ". . . We certainly do not want to become involved in a world struggle at any time," said General Marshall, "and certainly not prior to the time we are reasonably prepared to meet it."

The Soviet thrust in Korea had thus been directed at the point where we were weakest psychologically, at the gap between our all-out strategy, our forces-in-being and our inhibitions. It is remarkable that the Administration spokesmen were unanimous about our strategic superiority vis-à-vis the Soviet bloc, but they were also agreed that we must avoid all all-out war. The postulate that an all-out war had to be avoided short of an overt attack by the U.S.S.R. on us or on Europe was the reverse side of our inability to conceive goals of war other than the total defeat of the enemy. It represented an effort to elaborate a cause of war commensurate with the enormity of our weapons technology and with the only strategy we were prepared to pursue.

A Psychological Advantage

Given the threat which we knew the Soviet Union must soon pose when it had developed its nuclear capability further, it is possible to doubt the premise which lay behind the desire to avoid all-out war, the assumption that time was on our side, or at least to raise the question whether the U.S.S.R. did not have more to lose from an all-out war than we did. Be that as it may, our announced reluctance to engage in all-out war gave the Soviet bloc a psychological advantage. In the face of the inhibitions produced by our strategic doctrine, we tended to be more aware of our risks than of our opportunities; in fact, in our eyes even opportunities became risks. ". . . Russia possesses a very valuable ally in China," said General [George C.] Marshall. ". . . Now in view of their treaty with the Chinese Communist regime . . . if it appears that they have failed to support that government in its fight in Korea, we have a very special situation because it affects every other satellite of the Soviet. . . ." ". . . Whether or not the Soviet government can afford to have China defeated decisively by the Allies and put in a position where the reaction of China toward the Soviet Government might be one of deep distrust because they were not fully supported, that introduces a [new] factor in a current active situation. . . ." In short, we thought we could not afford to win in Korea, despite our strategic superiority, because Russia could not afford to lose.

A Policy of Limited Objectives

The Korean war was a peripheral war, therefore, not only because of its geographic location, but because of our difficulty in coming to grips with it. We kept it limited, not because we believed in limited war, but because we were reluctant to engage in all-out war over the issues which were at stake in Korea. Whatever aspects of the Korean war we considered—geographic location, strategy for conducting it, or our preparedness—we resolved them into arguments for keeping it to the smallest possible proportions.

As a result, many of the disputes produced by the Korean war were as abstract as the concept of power which produced them. They turned less on the opportunities presented by limited war than on the possibility of achieving all-out victory. MacArthur argued as if the Soviet timetable could not be affected by *any* measures the United States might take and that we could, therefore, crush China completely without fear of Soviet intervention. His opponents argued as if the U.S.S.R. were waiting for an excuse either to intervene in Asia or to launch forces against Western Europe.

By thus posing absolute alternatives as our only choices, by denying the existence of any middle ground between stalemate and total victory, both MacArthur and his opponents inhibited a consideration of strategic transformations which would be compatible with a policy of limited objectives. It was perhaps true that the U.S.S.R. would not permit an unambiguous defeat of China in an all-out war leading to the overthrow of the Communist regime. But it did not follow that the U.S.S.R. would risk everything in order to forestall *any* transformations in our favor, all the more so as our nuclear superiority was still very pronounced. Had we pushed back the Chinese armies even to the narrow neck of the Korean peninsula, we would have administered a setback to Communist power in its first trial at arms with the free world. This might have caused China to question the value of its Soviet alliance while the U.S.S.R. would have been confronted with the dilemma of whether it was "worth" an all-out war to prevent a limited defeat of its ally. A limited war is inconsistent with an attempt to impose unconditional surrender. But the impossibility of imposing unconditional surrender should not be confused with the inevitability of a return to the *status quo ante.*

Our strategic doctrine made it very difficult, however, to think of the possibility of intermediary transformations. Its defensive assumptions led us to analyze Soviet reactions as if every move were equally open to the Kremlin. And the divorce between force and diplomacy tended to paralyze both. The objective of our campaign was varyingly stated as repelling aggression, resisting aggression, punishing aggression, or as the security of our forces. Each of these objectives was defined in military terms and each assumed that diplomacy would take over only *after* a position of strength had been established.

The Korean war thus represented an application of the doctrine of containment. In fact, it was explicitly justified in those terms. But it suffered from the same drawbacks. Throughout the Korean war we made our objectives dependent on the military situation: they fluctuated with the fortunes of battle between repelling aggression, unification, the security of our forces, and a guaranteed armistice.

Negotiation Through Force
The fluctuation of our objectives demonstrated that it is impossible to conduct limited wars on the basis of purely military considerations. After [MacArthur's successful landing at] Inchon, at a moment of maximum strength, we proved unable to create a political framework for settling the Korean war, and we thereby provided the enemy with an incentive, if any was needed, to seek to restore the military balance as a prerequisite to any negotiation. It is not clear that a generous and comprehensive offer, for example, to

stop at the narrow neck of the peninsula and to demilitarize the rest of North Korea under United Nations supervision, would have been accepted; for purposes of this argument, it is sufficient to note that it was never made. The attempt by both sides to achieve a position of strength *prior* to negotiation resulted in a vicious circle of gradually expanding commitments which was brought to a halt only because an equilibrium was gradually established between the physical inability of Communist China to invest more resources in the conflict and our psychological unwillingness to do so.

The same attitude toward power which kept our diplomacy from setting limits to our military aims after we had the upper hand also prevented us from drawing strength from our military posture after we had opened negotiations for an armistice. Our decision to stop military operations, except those of a purely defensive nature, at the *very beginning* of the armistice negotiations reflected our conviction that the process of negotiation operated on its own inherent logic independently of the military pressures brought to bear. But by stopping military operations we removed the only Chinese incentive for a settlement; we produced the frustration of two years of inconclusive negotiations. In short, our insistence on divorcing force from diplomacy caused our power to lack purpose and our negotiations to lack force.

APPENDIX OF PERSONALITIES

Dean Acheson
As U.S. secretary of state under President Harry Truman from 1949 until 1952, Acheson helped create the Truman Doctrine and the Marshall Plan. He also played a key role in the formation of the North Atlantic Treaty Organization (NATO).

Charles E. Bohlen
Bohlen, an American diplomat, was considered an expert on Soviet affairs. Bohlen believed the Soviet Union did not intend to expand the war outside of Korea, a belief that came into conflict with the more unyieldingly hard-line politics of Secretary of State John Foster Dulles. Bohlen became ambassador to the Soviet Union in 1953 but was transferred to the Philippines as a result of his differences with Dulles.

Omar Bradley
A graduate of West Point, General Omar Nelson Bradley led the Normandy invasion during World War II. After the war, Bradley became the first permanent chairman of the Joint Chiefs of Staff in 1948. Two years later he would become general of the army, the highest-ranking officer in the army.

Winston Churchill
Churchill became prime minister of Great Britain after Neville Chamberlain was forced to resign in 1940. He led the nation through World War II and became recognized for his galvanizing speeches. After his political party was defeated in 1949, Churchill went to the United States to speak in Fulton, Missouri. He made a controversial speech

that would be among his most well known about the Soviet Union and the iron curtain.

Mark W. Clark

General Clark took over command of the Eighth Army after General Matthew Ridgway was promoted to UN commander. Clark became supreme commander in 1952. He was opposed to making concessions to the Communists and preferred to use the threat of military force to bring the Koreans to the peace talks.

John Foster Dulles

A lawyer and diplomat, Dulles was secretary of state under President Dwight D. Eisenhower from 1953 until 1959. Dulles helped to shape foreign policy. He believed communism was intrinsically evil and that collective security and the threat of a massive retaliation were the best ways to keep the Soviet Union in check.

Dwight D. Eisenhower

A former general who commanded Allied forces during World War II, Eisenhower became the thirty-fourth president of the United States in 1953. He helped put a quick end to the Korean War but continued to follow the U.S. policy of containment throughout his two terms.

C. Turner Joy

Vice Admiral Joy commanded the naval forces in Korea. He was chosen to be the chief delegate in charge of peace negotiations. His frustrations with Communist obstinacy led to his request to be reassigned.

George F. Kennan

Kennan was a State Department diplomat and the architect of Cold War containment policy. For years he was the chief adviser to Secretary of State Dean Acheson. In 1952 he became the ambassador to the Soviet Union but was recalled at the request of the Soviet government for unfavorable comments he made about Moscow.

Nikita Khrushchev

A secretary to the Central Committee of the Communist Party during the reign of Joseph Stalin in the 1930s, Khrushchev rose to power alongside Stalin. In 1939 he became a full member of the Politburo, the central governing body of the Communist Party. Georgy Malenkov succeeded Stalin as premier in 1953. But Khrushchev managed to unseat Malenkov and eventually became premier of the Soviet Union in 1958.

Henry A. Kissinger

Secretary of State Kissinger helped shape foreign policy under Presidents Richard Nixon and Gerald Ford from 1973 until 1977. Kissinger won the 1973 Nobel Peace Prize for his role in ending the Vietnam War. He also helped bring about a cease-fire in the Arab-Israeli War in 1973.

Douglas MacArthur

MacArthur is one of the most well-known American military leaders in history and is heralded for his victories in the war against Japan. MacArthur was appointed as commander of UN forces in Korea in 1950. He led UN forces to a sure victory with his amphibious landing at Inchon but misread the intentions of the Chinese, who sent troops into Korea. MacArthur insisted on attacking bases in China and using atomic weapons; he was relieved of his command because of his growing dissent with President Truman.

Georgy M. Malenkov

A former aide to Stalin, Malenkov became premier in 1953. Malenkov was known for his more conciliatory foreign policies toward the West. He was forced to resign in 1955 and was eventually expelled from the Communist Party in 1961.

Jacob Malik

Malik was the Soviet delegate to the UN. His absence (in protest) at the beginning of the Korean conflict allowed Truman to put forth a resolution condemning the North Koreans and calling for military intervention.

Syngman Rhee

The first president of the Republic of Korea (South Korea) from 1948 to 1960, Rhee was very vocal about uniting Korea and continued to campaign for this even after the war's end. He was eventually driven out of office by an outraged public that had had enough of Rhee's posturing and corrupt government. He was sent into exile and lived in Hawaii until his death.

Matthew B. Ridgway

General Ridgway, who led the Eighty-second Airborne troops during World War II, was given control of the Eighth Army in Korea in 1950. He was later given MacArthur's command of all UN forces after the controversial general's dismissal in 1951. Ridgway was able to turn the war around for the UN and drive the Communists back across the thirty-eighth parallel.

Franklin D. Roosevelt

Roosevelt was the former governor of New York and America's first three-term president (1932–1945). He led the nation through the Great Depression and World War II before dying in office in 1945.

Joseph Stalin

Stalin succeeded Vladimir Lenin as leader of the Communist Party and the Soviet Union. He was known as a ruthless leader who conducted widespread purges during the 1930s throughout the government and military to solidify his control. His death led to an easing of the tensions between the East and the West and a faster resolution to the Korean War.

Kim Il Sung

Sung led a resistance movement against the Japanese in occupied Manchuria during World War II. He later returned to Korea with the Red Army and became the first premier of the Democratic People's Republic in 1948. Sung made the decision on his own to reunify Korea by force. Although the invasion failed, Sung remained dictator of North Korea until his death in 1994.

Harry S. Truman

Truman was Franklin Roosevelt's vice president and succeeded Roosevelt after his death in 1945. He took office during one of the most difficult periods of U.S. history. Truman established the foreign policy of the United States that stood throughout the entire Cold War.

Mao Zedong (or Mao Tse-tung)

Founder of the Chinese Communist Party, Zedong became the first premier of the People's Republic of China in 1949. While in office he was able to influence Communist movements throughout the world. His writings were widely published and established him as one of the most influential political-military theorists in history.

CHRONOLOGY

1945

August 8: Adhering to a deal made with the United States, the Soviet Union enters the Pacific war and invades Japanese-occupied Manchuria and Korea.

August 11: Korea is divided at the thirty-eighth parallel into two occupation zones.

August 15: Japan agrees to surrender; World War II officially ends.

September 8: U.S. forces land in South Korea.

1947

March 12: President Truman requests funding for the Truman Doctrine, an assistance package for distressed European nations; the Marshall Plan, which encouraged mutual support among Western European nations, would be implemented months later.

July 26: Truman's National Security Act is passed, which creates the Department of Defense.

1948

June 24: The Soviet Union blocks all entry into Berlin in hopes of driving out the United States, Great Britain, and France; the United States responds with the Berlin Airlift, which brings food and supplies into the city by air.

August 15: The Republic of Korea (South Korea) is formed; Syngman Rhee is elected president; the United States turns over control to the new government.

September 9: The Democratic People's Republic of Korea (North Korea) is formed; Kim Il Sung is proclaimed premier of the new Communist government.

1949

April 4: The North Atlantic Treaty Organization (NATO) is formed.

July 14: The Soviet Union explodes its first atomic bomb; the balance of power is changed, escalating the Cold War.

October 1: China falls to Communist forces; party chairman Mao Zedong becomes the leader of the new People's Republic of China.

1950

June 25: North Korea invades South Korea in an attempt to reunify the country by force.

June 27: The United Nations calls for volunteer nations to assist South Korea.

June 28: North Korean forces capture the southern capital of Seoul.

June 30: President Truman orders U.S. ground forces into Korea and a naval blockade of the North Korean coast; he also authorizes the air force to conduct bombing missions.

July 1: The first U.S. troops are pulled from Japan and sent to Korea to delay the North Korean advance; they are quickly overwhelmed.

July 8: General Douglas MacArthur is declared supreme commander of UN forces in Korea.

August 1: Outnumbered U.S. and South Korean forces are driven back to the coast by the advancing North Korean army; the allies establish a defensive line called the Pusan Perimeter.

September 15: General MacArthur leads a daring amphibious assault at the port city of Inchon behind enemy lines.

September 16: UN forces break out of the Pusan Perimeter to meet with MacArthur; the defeated North Korean army is soon driven back across the thirty-eighth parallel.

September 27: Seoul is recaptured; General MacArthur is given permission to cross the thirty-eighth parallel into North Korea.

October 2: After repeated warnings threatening intervention if the UN invade North Korea, the Chinese decide to enter the war.

October 14: Chinese forces cross the Yalu River at the Korean border.

October 19: North Korea's capital, Pyongyang, is captured by UN forces.

October 24: MacArthur orders Allied forces to the Yalu River.

November 25: After UN forces reach the Manchurian border, MacArthur promises troops they will be "home by Christmas" if the offensive is successful.

November 25–28: The Chinese launch a counterattack with two hundred thousand troops.

November 30: The use of atomic weapons is not ruled out by Truman at a press conference.

December 25: UN forces are driven back across the thirty-eighth parallel.

December 30: The U.S. air force encounters Russian-made MiG 15 fighters near the Yalu River in the first battle between jet aircraft.

1951

January 1: A new Communist offensive begins.

January 5: Communist forces recapture Seoul.

January 25: UN forces begin a new offensive named Operation Thunderbolt.

February 11: UN forces again cross the thirty-eighth parallel.

February 22: General Matthew Ridgway's counteroffensive, Operation Killer, begins.

March 15: UN forces recapture Seoul.

April 11: Truman relieves MacArthur of command for insubordination; General Ridgway is given his command.

June 23: The Soviet Union proposes truce talks.

July 10: Truce talks begin at Kaesong.

August 23: Truce talks are suspended on charges of violation of the neutral zone; negotiations resume two months later at nearby Panmunjom.

1952

May 7: POW repatriation becomes an impasse at the peace talks.

May 12: Ridgway replaces General Dwight D. Eisenhower as supreme commander of Allied forces in Europe; General Mark Clark succeeds Ridgway as supreme UN commander.

November 4: Eisenhower is elected president of the United States; during his campaign, he promises a quick end to the Korean War.

1953

March 5: Soviet dictator Joseph Stalin dies; new premier Georgy Malenkov believes the East and the West can peacefully coexist and gives the stalled peace talks new impetus.

July 27: The armistice agreement is signed at Panmunjom.

1958

October 26: Chinese troops withdraw from Korea; they commit over two hundred violations of the armistice agreement.

FOR FURTHER RESEARCH

Books

Bevin Alexander, *Korea: The First War We Lost*. New York: Hippocrene Books, 1986.

Henry Berry, *Hey, Mac, Where Ya Been? Living Memories of the U.S. Marines in the Korean War*. New York: St. Martin's, 1988.

Charles E. Bohlen, *Witness to History: 1929–1969*. New York: W.W. Norton, 1973.

James Bradey, *The Coldest War*. New York: Orion Books, 1990.

Omar N. Bradley and Clay Blair, *A General's Life*. New York: Simon and Schuster, 1983.

Edward Crankshaw, *Khrushchev Remembers*. Boston: Little, Brown, 1970.

John Dille, *Substitute for Victory*. Garden City, NY: Doubleday, 1954.

Peter G. Filene, ed., *American Views of Soviet Russia: 1917–1965*. Homewood, IL: Dorsey, 1968.

Allan E. Goodman, ed., *Negotiating While Fighting: The Diary of Admiral C. Turner Joy at the Korean Armistice Conference*. Stanford, CA: Hoover Institution, 1978.

Allen Guttmann, ed., *Korea, Cold War and Limited War*. Lexington, MA: D.C. Heath, 1972.

Marguerite Higgins, *War in Korea: The Report of a Woman Combat Correspondent*. Garden City, NY: Doubleday, 1951.

Burton I. Kaufman, *The Korean Conflict*. Westport, CT: Greenwood, 1999.

Henry A. Kissinger, *Nuclear Weapons and Foreign Policy.* New York: Harper & Brothers, 1957.

Xiaobing Li, Allan R. Millett, and Bin Yu, eds. and translators, *Mao's Generals Remember Korea.* Lawrence: University Press of Kansas, 2001.

Y.T. Pyun, *Korea—My Country.* Washington, DC: Korean Pacific, 1953.

David Rees, *Korea: The Limited War.* New York: St. Martin's, 1964.

Syngman Rhee, *The Spirit of Independence: A Primer of Korean Modernization and Reform.* Honolulu: University of Hawai'i Press, 2001.

Matthew B. Ridgway, *The Korean War.* New York: Doubleday, 1967.

John W. Riley Jr. and Wilbur Schramm, *The Reds Take a City: The Communist Occupation of Seoul.* New Brunswick, NJ: Rutgers University Press, 1951.

Senate Committee on the Judiciary, Subcommittee to Investigate the Administration of the Internal Security Act and Other Internal Security Laws, *The Korean War and Related Matters*, 84th Congress, January 21, 1955.

James Samuel Stemons, *The Korean Mess: And Some Correctives.* Boston: Chapman and Grimes, 1952.

Kim Il Sung, *Kim Il Sung for the Independent, Peaceful Reunification of Korea.* New York: International, 1975.

John Toland, *In Mortal Combat: Korea, 1950–1953.* New York: William Morrow, 1991.

Rudy Tomedi, *No Bugles, No Drums: An Oral History of the Korean War.* New York: John Wiley & Sons, 1993.

U.S. Operations Research Office, *Beliefs of Enemy Soldiers About the Korean War.* Baltimore, MD: U.S. Operations Research Office, Johns Hopkins University, 1952.

A Volunteer Soldier's Day: Recollections by Men of the Chinese People's Volunteers in the War to Resist U.S.

Aggression and Aid Korea. Peking: Foreign Language, 1961.

Courtney Whitney, *MacArthur, His Rendezvous with History*. New York: Alfred A. Knopf, 1956.

Larry Zellers, *In Enemy Hands: A Prisoner in North Korea*. Lexington: University Press of Kentucky, 1991.

Periodical

Department of State Bulletin, July 3–November 25, 1950; March 5, 1951; March 19, 1951; April 16, 1951.

Website

Library of Congress, www.loc.gov.

INDEX

74–75, 108–109
on demarcation line, 179,
180
detering imperialism of,
34–35
Eastern Bloc countries
and, 14
foreign policy of, vs. U.S.
foreign policy, 63
negotiations with the U.S.,
28–30
North Korean and
Chinese prisoners of war
on, 130–32
proposal for a truce, 178
psychological advantage
of, 216–17
reasons for South Korean
attack, 50–51
as recognizing only force,
105
role in invasion of South
Korea, 20, 48–49
direct involvement,
57–58
vs. Korean civil war,
63–65
Stalin's motives, 55–57
as strategy for world
domination, 35–38
was not a forerunner to
future invasions, 54–55
separation of Korea and,
18
threat of Communist
expansion by, 44–45
U.S. cooperation with, 46
con, 46–47

see also communism/
Communists; Stalin,
Joseph
Stalin, Joseph
Berlin and, 16
motives for South Korean
invasion, 55–57
on North Korean invasion
of South Korea, 20
strategy to expand
communism, 44–45
Yalta Conference and,
17–18
see also Soviet Union
Stemons, James Samuel, 62
Strategic Air Force, 41

Tai Ching-Shan, 162
Taiwan, 85–86
Task Force Smith, 21, 155
Truman, Harry S., 91
on achievement of peace,
97–98
aid to Greece and Turkey
and, 15
China and, 66
on Communist plan for
world conquest, 93–94
on Communist threat,
91–92
decision to involve U.S. in
Korean War, 38
helping to stop
Communist expansion,
59–60
influence of Dean
Acheson on, 60
MacArthur and, 27, 97